现代职业教育体

Business Communication

商务沟通

上册

主　　编：黎云莺

副主编：吴　磊

参　　编：朱艳君　　陈晓峰

　　　　　杨宇晖　　凌　燕

广东高等教育出版社

Guangdong Higher Education Press

广州

图书在版编目（CIP）数据

商务沟通. 上册/黎云莺主编. —广州：广东高等教育出版社，
2014.8

（现代职业教育体系培育教材）

ISBN 978 - 7 - 5361 - 5146 - 8

Ⅰ. ①商…　Ⅱ. ①黎…　Ⅲ. ①商业管理 - 公共关系学 - 高等
职业教育 - 教材　Ⅳ. ①F715

中国版本图书馆 CIP 数据核字（2014）第 133976 号

商务沟通
Shangwu Goutong

广东高等教育出版社出版发行
地址：广州市天河区林和西横路
邮编：510500　电话：（020）87553735
http://www.gdgjs.com.cn
广州市穗彩印务有限公司印刷
787 毫米×1 092 毫米　16 开本　11.25 印张　238 千字
2014 年 8 月第 1 版　2014 年 8 月第 1 次印刷
印数：1~2 000 册
定价：29.00 元（随书附送光盘）

前　言

　　《商务沟通》是由广东高等教育出版社出版的面向 21 世纪的商务英语专业三二分段中高职衔接教材。本书运用以学生为本位和项目驱动相结合的方法，按照"简明实用，易懂易练，培养职业技能，提升职业素养"的原则进行编写。本书共 20 个单元（模块），分上、下两册，内容编排由浅入深，基本上涵盖了日常商务活动中基本的商务沟通情景，如商务沟通中的商务交际、商务会话、商务会议、商务英语演讲等。

　　本着在商务环境中学习英语、增长商务知识和提高技能的宗旨，秉承工学结合、以学生为本位的教学理念，本书将实际工作岗位的技能要求模块化，采取任务驱动的形式，按照"简明实用，易懂易练，培养职业技能，提升职业素养"的原则进行编写。本书适合中高职商务英语专业的学生作为专业课程教材使用，也适合国际商务、国际贸易、国际企业管理和涉外文秘等涉及商务交际活动的学生和社会人员使用。

　　全书以同一个主人公 Kary 的职场经历和工作成长过程，把 20 个单元的内容串起来，以讲故事的形式展示内容，练习中可以让学生扮演主人公。每个单元的具体内容包括：

　　【Learning Objectives】即场景和本章的学习目标。介绍主人公所面对的商务场景和需要完成的任务，150～200 字。

　　【Warming-up】完成任务所需要的知识。请同学们假设自己是主人公，思考完成任务和对话中可能会遇到的问题。课本列举出相关知识，主要包括词汇、常用句型等。

　　【Kary's Story】与单元主题相关的英语对话 2～3 篇。学生就对话内容或视频内容回答问题或完成任务。

　　【Listening Practice】听力练习 1～2 题。

　　【Culture Note】涉外文化背景介绍或跨文化交际的商务沟通礼仪等。

　　【Pair Work】两人一组的课堂练习。

【Socializing Practice】课后练习，2～4题。

【Daily Practice】语音训练材料。

本教材由黎云莺、吴磊主编，多所中高职院校经验丰富的教学一线教师参与了本书的编写。其中上册由吴磊编写第1、9单元，杨宇晖编写第2、4单元，朱艳君编写第3、5单元，陈晓峰编写第6、7单元，凌燕编写第8、10单元。下册由王娜编写第1、10单元，黎云莺编写第2、3单元，冯敏贤编写第4、5单元，蒋琳编写第6、9单元，迟雯编写第7、8单元。

本书在编写过程中参考了国内外出版的一些教材，获益良多，编者在此谨对本书参考的教材、专著和网络素材的版权所有者表示衷心的感谢。

由于时间仓促，编者水平有限，书中缺点、错漏之处在所难免，希望专家和使用者批评指正。

编　者

2013 年 10 月

CONTENTS

Unit 1 　Interviewing a Job ·· (1)

Unit 2 　Greeting and Introduction ································· (16)

Unit 3 　Making More Contacts with Strangers ················· (30)

Unit 4 　Communicating with Colleagues ····················· (43)

Unit 5 　Communicating with Customers ····················· (57)

Unit 6 　Making Reservation and Appointments ·············· (69)

Unit 7 　Dealing with Daily Affairs ······························ (84)

Unit 8 　Socializing after Work ·································· (101)

Unit 9 　Non-verbal Communication ···························· (114)

Unit 10 　Making Farewells ······································ (127)

Appendix I 　New Words and Expressions ···················· (139)

Appendix II 　Reference Answers ······························· (146)

Appendix III 　Listening Scripts ································· (164)

Bibliography ·· (172)

Unit 1 Interviewing a Job

Learning Objectives

Kary is going to take a job interview and give a brief self-introduction. Kary's objectives are to master the basic words, expressions and useful sentences of interviewing a job; to learn the skills of making an effective preparation for the job interview and to design her own resume. Kary's experiences will guide you to know the general questions and procedure of English interview and lead you to a successful performance for your own interview.

Warming-up

1. **What do you think can make a successful interview?**

( ) formal wear   ( ) a well-designed resume[①]
( ) a good appearance[②]   ( ) good communication skills
( ) a graceful manner   ( ) to arrive on time
( ) smile   ( ) educational background
( ) work experience   ( ) politeness

2. **List some troublesome questions in a job interview and try to answer these questions properly.**

Kary's Story

Dialogue 1   Job Interview

The month before graduation, as other students, Kary is busy hunting a job. Now she prepares to take an interview at the job market. She knocks at the door and waits for the signal of the interviewer.

(K = Kary; J = John Smith, the interviewer)

---

① resume 简历
② appearance 外貌，外表

J：Come in, please.

K：Thank you.

J：I'm John Smith, Personnel Manager[①] of the company.

K：My name is Kary. How do you do, Mr. Smith?

J：How do you do, Kary? Now let's get down to the interview. May I ask you some personal questions?

K：Certainly.

J：When and where were you born?

K：I was born in 1990 and was brought up in Guangzhou.

J：Can you tell me something about your family?

K：Yes. I have a happy and cozy family. There are four people in my family：my parents, my younger brother and myself. My parents are in their fifties, and they are both teachers. My younger brother is at college.

J：What kind of hobbies do you have?

K：I'm fond of reading, sports and travelling.

J：What kind of personality do you think you have?

K：I think I am quite outgoing, sociable, adaptable[②] and hard-working.

J：Do you have any special skills or other qualifications?

K：I am proficient in English and can speak fluent Mandarin[③], Cantonese and a little French.

J：Can you use a computer?

K：Yes, I'm familiar with such software as Windows 7, Microsoft Word, Excel, and Powerpoint.

J：Why did you choose our company?

K：Two weeks ago, I read your advertisement in *Guangzhou Daily*. Your company is a famous multi-national corporation. I'm sure I would be able to better develop my abilities if I had a chance to work for your company.

J：What starting salary would you expect?

K：I would expect the appropriate rate of pay for a person with my experience and educational background.

J：I see. So much for the interview, we will contact you later if you are taken in. Thanks for your cooperation.

K：It's my pleasure.

---

① personnel manager 人事经理

② adaptable 适应性强的

③ Mandarin 普通话

▶ Useful sentences

1. Now let's get down to the interview.

现在让我们开始面试。

2. May I ask you some personal questions?

我能了解一下你的个人情况吗?

3. What kind of personality do you think you have?

你认为你的性格如何?

4. Do you have any special skills or other qualifications?

你有什么特长和其他过人之处吗?

5. I am proficient in English.

我擅长英语。

6. Your company is a famous multi-national corporation.

贵公司是一家有名的跨国公司。

7. I would expect the appropriate rate of pay for a person with my experience and educational background.

我希望能拿到和我的工作经验和学历相称的薪酬等级。

▶ Other useful sentences

1. recommendation letter 推荐信

A recommendation letter from Professor Li sometimes is helpful when you want to get a job in this field.

如果你想在这个领域找工作的话,李教授的推荐信也许有帮助。

2. personal information 个人信息

Your CV should include six different areas of information: personal information, education and qualifications, work experience, interests and achievements, skills and referees.

简历需要覆盖六个方面的信息:个人基本信息、教育背景和资格证书、工作经历、兴趣和成就、技能和推荐人。

3. interest and speciality 兴趣与特长

My interest and speciality: Love basketball and football heartily, like to participate in the group activity.

我的兴趣与特长如下:热爱篮球和足球,喜欢参加团体活动。

4. honor and award 荣誉和奖励

Did you get any honors or awards at college?

你大学时获过什么荣誉和奖励吗?

5. professional certificate 职业技能证书

Your application should include all relevant information, such as the position you would like to apply for, a resume, professional certificates and photos.

你的书面申请书应该包括你所有的重要信息，如你希望应聘的职位、简历、职业技能证书以及个人照片。

Tips：

Read the following tips for preparing an interview.

1. Do some research ahead so you'll know something about the company and the position①. This will help you answer questions and impress the interviewer.

2. Show up for the interview with well-dressed clothes. A suit and tie is the appropriate dress. Make sure the suit is clean and pressed by a cleaner.

3. Shake hands with the interviewer in a proper way. Most westerners prefer a strong handshake, but fairly brief, perhaps two or three seconds.

4. Remember the interviewer's name, so you can use it throughout the interview. Call them Mr. or Ms.

5. Answer questions honestly. Experienced interviewers can often tell when you're not honest.

6. Take a moment to organize your thoughts before answering difficult questions.

7. Look at the interviewer in the eyes when introducing yourself, and frequently when answering questions. Westerners like eye contact.

8. Show enthusiasm② for the company and the job. Companies want to hire people who show great interest and want to be there!

Dialogue 2

Kary will take another interview and apply for the position of the foreign trade salesperson.

(K = Kary; G = Gary Henson, the interviewer)

G：Good morning, I'm Gary Henson. Please take a seat.

K：Good morning, I'm Kary, nice to meet you.

G：Nice to meet you, too. To start with, can you tell me why you are interested in working for our company?

K：Because your company has a great future and I'll be able to develop my own capabilities here.

---

① position 职位，岗位

② enthusiasm 热情

G: I see. Which university did you graduate from? And what is your major?

K: I graduated from Guangdong Foreign Trade School and my major is Business English.

G: What were your scores at college?

K: They were all above average.

G: Did you get any honors or awards at your university?

K: I won the university scholarship for four years on end.

G: How would you describe your personality?

K: I am tolerant①, slow to anger, tactful②, caring and friendly.

G: What are some of your strong and weak points?

K: Well, I suppose a strong point of mine is that I like developing new things and ideas. But I'm afraid I'm a poor talker and that isn't very good, so I've been studying how to speak in public.

G: What sort of work experience do you have?

K: When I was at college, I worked as a receptionist at a four-star hotel during my summer vacation.

G: Do you think the work experience is helpful for the position you apply for?

K: I met all kinds of people around the world every day and answered their questions, it made me more patient and improve my communication skills and social experience. Now I think I can get along very well with others and communicate well with my business partners in my future work.

G: What's your expectation on this job?

K: Except for the enriching work experience and the salary, I also expect to learn more about other countries with their cultures and their attitudes toward life.

G: Very well. So, where do you see yourself in five or ten years?

K: If I'm lucky enough to have this position, I'll endeavor to know whatever a foreign trade salesperson should know and hopefully move into an experienced one step by step.

G: All right. If you get the job, when can you start?

K: Next Monday would be good for me.

G: OK. Glad to talk to you today. We'll notify③ you of our decision within a week. Goodbye.

① tolerant 宽容的，容忍的

② tactful 机智的，老练的

③ notify 通知

K：I'll look forward to it. Thank you for your interview with me, sir. Goodbye.

▶ **Useful sentences**

1. My major is Business English.

我的专业是商务英语。

2. They were all above average.

各科成绩均中等偏上。

3. Did you get any honors or awards at your university?

你在大学曾获得哪些荣誉和奖项？

4. I won the university scholarship for four years on end.

我连续四年获得奖学金。

5. I worked as a receptionist at a four-star hotel during my summer vacation.

在暑假期间，我曾在一家四星级宾馆担任前台服务员。

6. I'll endeavor to know whatever a foreign trade salesperson should know.

我会努力去熟悉一个外贸业务员应了解的业务内容。

Dialogue 3　A brief self-introduction

Good morning！

It is really my honor to have this opportunity① for an interview, I hope I can make a good performance and succeed today. Now I will introduce myself briefly. I am 23 years old, born in Guangdong province. I graduated from Guangdong Foreign Trade School. My major is Electronic Business and I got my Bachelor's degree after my graduation in the year of 2012. I have spent most of my time on study, and I have passed CET 4/6 and have acquired basic knowledge of my major during my school time. In July 2012, I began to work for a small private company as a documentation specialist in Shenzhen. Because I'm capable of more responsibilities②, I decided to change my job. Because I want to change my working environment, I'd like to find a job which has more challenges. Moreover, your company is a famous multi-national corporation, so I think I can gain the most from working in this kind of company environment. That is the reason why I come here to compete for this position. I think I'm a good team player and I'm a person of great honesty to others. Also I am able to work under pressure.

That's all. Thank you for giving me the chance.

――――――――――――

① opportunity 机会

② responsibility 责任，职责

▶ Useful sentences

1. I got my Bachelor's degree after my graduation in the year of 2012.

本人于 2012 年毕业，获得学士学位。

2. I have acquired basic knowledge of my major during my school time.

在求学期间，通过学习我掌握了本专业的基础知识。

3. I began to work for a small private company as a documentation specialist in Shenzhen.

刚开始我在深圳一家小型私企里担任单证员。

4. I'd like to find a job which has more challenges.

我想找一份更具挑战性的工作。

5. Moreover, your company is a famous multi-national corporation, so I think I can gain the most from working in this kind of company environment.

此外，贵公司是著名的跨国公司，我认为在这种企业氛围中工作会使我受益匪浅。

6. I am able to work under pressure.

本人具备较强的抗压能力。

Listening Practice

You are going to listen to two conversations about job interview and finish task A and B.

Task A：Decide which of these statements are true and which are false. Tick the correct box. If the statement is false，explain why it is wrong.

(   ) 1. The woman wants to get the job because she can make more money.

(   ) 2. The woman has a lot of work experience for this job.

(   ) 3. The woman is good at learning.

(   ) 4. She doesn't need any training for the job.

(   ) 5. The man would like to give the answer to the woman's application[①] the next day.

Task B：Questions 1 to 4 are based on the conversation you've heard.

1. In which department is Kary likely to work?

Kary is likely to work in _____.

2. Why is Kary willing to get the position?

Because she _____.

---

① application 申请表，申请书

3. What's the special requirement for the job?

Kary is required to _____.

4. How long does it take Kary to get to the company by bus?

It only takes _____.

Culture Note

Some "Dos" and "Don'ts" in the job interview

"Dos":

1. Do plan to arrive on time or a few minutes early. Late arrival for a job interview is never excusable①.

2. If you present an application, do fill it out neatly and completely. You can not rely on application or resume to do the selling for you. Interviewers will want you to speak for yourself.

3. Do greet the interviewer by last name if you know how to read it. If not, ask the interviewer to repeat it. Shake hands firmly and show your pleasure to meet the interviewer.

4. Do wait until you are offered a chair before sitting. Sit upright, look relaxed and interested at all times. Be a good listener as well as a good talker.

5. Do look at prospective② employer in the eyes while speaking.

6. Do follow the interviewer's leads, but try to get the interviewer to describe the position and the duties to you early in the interview so that you can apply your background, skills and work experience to the position.

7. Do make sure that your good points come across to the interviewer in an honest, sincere manner. Try to stress your achievements③. For example: sales records, a piece of successful work, the awards you got, etc.

8. Do always make as if to decide to get the job you are discussing. Never close the door on purpose.

9. Do show enthusiasm. If you are interested in the opportunity, your enthusiastic feedback④ can bring you more chances to get the job.

"Don'ts":

1. Don't forget to bring a copy of your resume. Keep several copies in your briefcase if

---

① excusable 可辩解的，可原谅的

② prospective 预期的，未来的

③ achievement 成就，业绩

④ feedback 回应，反馈

you are afraid you will forget.

2. Don't smoke, even if the interviewer does and offers you a cigarette.

3. Do not chew gum.

4. Don't answer questions with a simple "yes" or "no". Explain the reasons if it is possible. Describe those things about yourself which relate to the situation.

5. Don't over-answer questions. And if the interviewer turns the conversation into politics or controversial[①] topics, try to do more listening than speaking.

6. Don't make unnecessary derogatory remarks[②] about your present or former employers. When explaining your reasons for leaving, just give your own reasons why you want to get a new job.

7. Don't ask too much about the payment at the beginning of the interview unless you are sure the employer is interested in hiring you. If the interviewer asks directly about your expected salary, you can tell him clearly the payment you want to get.

Pair Work

1. **Discuss with your partner and give your judgment and reasons on the questions related to job interview preparations.**

1) Is it possible to guess the questions of a job interview?

2) Will the interviewer check the information on an applicant's application?

3) Should the candidate[③] tell the interviewer how wonderful he/she is?

4) When having a job interview, should the applicant give real examples to answer the questions?

5) Should the candidate wear formally in a job interview?

2. **Imagine you're just entering into your first job interview in English. Talk with a partner. Answer the following questions.**

1) What job might you be seeking?

2) What research should you do before the interview to make it go well for you?

3) How should you show up[④] for your interview?

4) What kind of handshake do most westerners prefer?

---

① controversial 有争议的

② derogatory remark 贬损的评价

③ candidate 应聘者，候选人

④ show up 露面，出现

5）When should you look the interviewer in the eyes?

6）Why should you remember the interviewer's name?

7）What should you do before answering difficult questions?

8）Why should you show enthusiasm for the job?

3. Make notes from dialogue 1 ~ 3 and try to give a brief self-introduction for your job interview. Your self-introduction should include the following contents：personal information，education background，work experience，specialty，professional certificates. The useful sentences in the above dialogues may help you to organize your structure.

Socializing Practice

▶ Role-play

An interview will be conducted between employer（Student A）and employee（Student B）. After 10 minutes Student A and Student B will change their roles.

Task 1

Student A：

You work for a clothing company and want to recruit① some energetic，youthful people to your market department. Experience is not so important，but enthusiasm and the desire to learn is.

Student B：

You have applied for a clothing company that wants to recruit some energetic，youthful people to its market department. You are keen on the job，and think you may have a chance because they say that experience is not so important，but enthusiasm and the desire to learn is. Give student A your curriculum vitae② to read，then prepare to be interviewed by her/him. Prepare a list of subjects that you think the interviewer might ask and plan how to "sell" yourself at the interview.

Task 2

Student A：

Suppose you are the owner of a Korean restaurant in Sydney. You are seeking to hire an experienced Korean Head Chef③ to work in your kitchen and plan to host the job interview for

---

① recruit 招收

② curriculum vitae 简历，履历

③ Korean Head Chef 韩式料理首席厨师

the applicants. To assure the high-class quality of food and service, you fix the prerequisites[①] for this position:

1) Must have at least 2 years' experience as a chef because the person will be in charge of the kitchen.

2) Must speak fluent English and Korean.

3) Must have recognized training in preparing Korean food from a reputable cooking academy[②].

4) Must be looking for a long-term position.

5) Must be able to work in Australia.

You may use the possible interview questions that you have learned to help you. After the interview, you are required to make a presentation[③] to explain who you would like to hire and why.

Student B:

You will act as one of the following applicants and make a short presentation about your personal information, work experience and qualifications.

Jobseeker 1 (Male):

Your name is Robin and you are an experienced Korean chef. You are 55 years old. You have been living in Sydney since you were ten and learnt to cook Korean food from your mother and then from the Sydney school of Korean Cuisine[④]. You used to have your own Korean restaurant in Sydney's south side but you sold it, because you are getting older. You are hoping to retire in ten years. You speak English better than Korean but still speak Korean.

Jobseeker 2 (Female):

Your name is Tim Chung and you are 30 years old. You are Korean and are in Australia on a two-year work visa. You are from Busan and have worked in a Korean restaurant in Busan for ten years before you came over to Australia. You studied Korean Cuisine at the Seoul Centre for Culinary Arts[⑤]. In the Korean restaurant, your job was Second Chef and you left the job because you want to be a Head Chef. You are hoping to get a job in Australia so you can extend your visa and move to Australia.

---

① prerequisite 先决条件

② reputable cooking academy 著名的烹饪院校

③ make a presentation 演示，表演

④ cuisine 烹饪方法，菜肴

⑤ culinary arts 烹饪艺术，厨艺

Jobseeker 3 （Male）:

Your name is Peter McDonald and you are 35 years old. You are a Canadian who has been crazy about Korean food since teaching English in Korea. You learnt to cook Korean food formally① at the Toronto College of Cuisine and have worked in a Korean restaurant in Toronto for 5 years. For 2 of the 5 years you were the Head Chef there. However, you quitted the job because you had an argument② with the restaurant owner over the menu. You decided to move to Australia because it is warmer and you want to work there for at least a year. You're not sure if you are going to live there for a long time. You speak English as the first language and have studied Korean in Korea for two years.

Jobseeker 4 （Female）:

Your name is Tina Kim and you graduated from Korean Cuisine College of Melbourne. You are 24 years old. You are ambitious③ and want to work as a Head Chef in a Korean restaurant but don't have experience. You have worked at the Melbourne Casino④ as a chef for two years. You have are an Australian citizen but you were born in Korea. You have moved to Sydney from Melbourne with your boyfriend for his job. You speak fluent Korean and English. Your boss at the Casino praised your hard-work and dedication⑤.

Some other qualities may make your presentation more persuasive⑥:

1. Possessing leadership qualities in character.
2. Having experience working in a Korean restaurant.
3. You are organized, efficient, punctual and hard-working.
4. Being able to build good relationships with co-workers.

Task 3: How to make your own "resume"?

Resume plays a very important role in hunting a job. It is just like your name card from which the interviewers know who you are, what you can do, how they can contact you and even your ways of doing things. A well-designed resume may be one of the stepping stones⑦ to a desirable job.

---

① formally 正式地

② argument 争论，争吵

③ ambitious 有雄心的

④ Melbourne Casino 墨尔本娱乐城

⑤ dedication 奉献精神

⑥ persuasive 有说服力的

⑦ stepping stone 敲门砖，垫脚石

Resume

Danni Liu
Female
International Economics and Trade
since 2006.1

2006 graduate of SWUFE

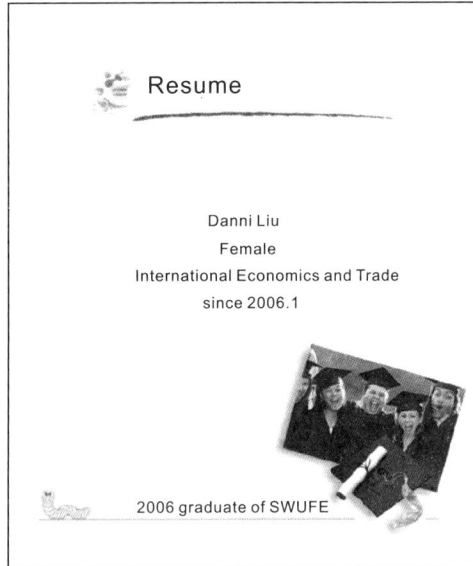

Chinese Name		Sex		Birthplace		
English Name		Telephone		Email		
University				Major		
Address						
Job Objective						
Computer Skills						
English Proficiency						
Education Experience						
Work Experience						

There are six main parts of resume:

1. Cover, including your name, major, mobile phone number, e-mail address and well-designed background picture.

2. Self-recommendation letter or a recommendation letter from your advisor.

3. Personal information including the following items: name, gender, birthplace,

age，address，interest and hobby，educational background.

4．A four-year mark sheet stamped by the office of teaching affairs[①].

5．Several significant certificates and professional qualifications.

6．Your acknowledgement[②] and future plan for the new job.

Practice

Design our own English resume according to the above format and try to polish it as well as you can.

Daily Practice

Tongue twister

1．A bloke's back bike brake block broke.

一个家伙的脚踏车后制动器坏了。

2．Mike likes to write by the bright light at night.

麦克喜欢夜晚在一盏明亮的灯下写作。

3．I scream，you scream，we all scream for ice cream！

我叫喊，你叫喊，我们都喊着要冰淇淋！

4．Can you imagine an imaginary menagerie manager imagining managing an imaginary menagerie?

你可以想象一个虚构的野生动物园经理幻想自己管理一个虚构的野生动物园吗?

5．When a doctor doctors another doctor，does he doctor the doctored doctor the way the doctored doctor wants to be doctored or does he doctor the doctored doctor the way the doctoring doctor wants to doctor the doctor?

如果一个医生给另一位医生看病，这个医生是按照来看病的医生想要被医治的方式还是按照自己想要医治的方式给来看病的医生治疗呢?

6．Betty bought some butter，but the butter Betty bought was bitter，so Betty bought some better butter，and the better butter Betty bought was better than the bitter butter Betty bought before！

贝蒂买了些黄油，但贝蒂买的黄油是苦的，所以贝蒂买了点更好的黄油，贝蒂买的好黄油比贝蒂之前买的苦黄油更好！

Read aloud

Self-introduction for the Interview of Postgraduate Recruitment

Good morning, my name is Jack. It is really a great honor to have this opportunity for

---

① the office of teaching affairs 教务部门

② acknowledgement 感谢，致谢

such an interview. I would like to answer whatever you may raise, and I hope I can make a good performance today. My major is packaging engineering and I will receive my bachelor degree after my graduation in June. In the past 4 years, I have spent most of my time on study, and I have passed CET6 with an ease and I have acquired basic knowledge of packaging and publishing both in theory and in practice. Besides, I have attended several packaging exhibitions held in Beijing, and this is our advantage study here. I guess you may be interested in the reason why I turn to maths, and what is my plan during postgraduate study life. I would like to tell you that pursuing maths is one of my lifelong goal. I like my packaging major and I won't give up. If I can pursue my master's degree here, I will combine maths with my former education.

As to my character, I cannot describe it well, but I know I am optimistic and confident. Through my college life, I learn how to balance between study and entertainment. By the way, I was an actor of our school drama club. I had a few glorious memories on stage and that is my pride. I sincerely hope that I can get the opportunity to have my further study in the kingdom of maths. Please give me a chance. I will work hard and make progress step by step.

Thank you!

Unit 2   Greeting and Introduction

Learning Objectives

Kary is going to report to the manager. Kary's objectives are to show us how to exchange greetings, introduce herself and introduce other colleagues. Kary's experience will let us know how to greet each other and make introduction on some formal occasions.

Warming-up

1. **How do you greet the new employees if you have been the staff in the company for some time**?

a. in the office　　　b. coffee time at work　　　c. after work

2. **How do the managers of departments introduce the new colleagues to other staff**?

a. When and where will the manager introduce the new staff?

b. What kind of things will the manager do?

c. How can the manager make the new staff be familiar with his/her working place and partners?

Kary's Story

Dialogue 1   Report to the Company

(K = Kary, the new staff of the company; S = Secretary, the receptionist of the company; L = Miss Lin, the manager of the Personnel Department)

S: Can I help you?

K: Yes. Would you tell me where I can find the Personnel Manager, Miss Lin?

S: Did you have an appointment① with her?

K: Yes, I am the new comer here. My name is Kary Zhang and I am asked to report② to her.

S: Welcome to our company, Kary. The manager is waiting for you. Her office is the second one on your left.

K: Thank you very much for your help.

(in Miss Lin's office)

L: Nice to meet you, Kary. Was there any trouble for you to find my office?

K: Not really. Shall I begin my job now?

L: Not so hurry. Let me introduce the main departments to you first.

K: OK. Thank you.

▶ Useful sentences

1. Would you tell me where I can find the Personnel Manager, Miss Lin?

---

① appointment 约会

② report 报到

你能告诉我在哪可以找到人事经理林小姐吗？

2. Did you have an appointment with her?

你和她有约吗？

3. I am asked to report to her.

我是来向她报到的。

4. Was there any trouble for you to find my office?

你找到我的办公室困难吗？

▶ Other useful sentences

1. May I introduce myself? I'm Kary from Shanghai.

我可以做一下自我介绍吗？我是来自上海的凯莉。

2. It's a pleasure to meet you. I'm Alice.

很高兴认识你。我是爱丽丝。

3. Would you tell me where the manager's office is?

请告诉我经理办公室在哪？

4. Pleased to meet you. My name is Helen.

很高兴见到你。我叫海伦。

5. How do you do? I'm Tom from Zhejiang University.

你好。我是来自浙江大学的汤姆。

6. Did you have any difficulty finding my office?

我的办公室难找吗？

7. What do you wish to see him about?

你找他有什么事吗？

8. Hello, let me introduce myself. My name is Wang Feng.

你好，让我自我介绍一下。我叫王峰。

9. Yes, that's him. Let me introduce you.

来了，他就在那，让我为你介绍一下。

10. I've just started work for IBM. I'm in the Sales Department.

我刚来 IBM 工作，在销售部。

11. I'm on the market research side. And you?

我是搞市场调研的。你呢？

12. Pleased to meet you. I'm Jackson Black. I haven't seen you around before.

很高兴认识你，我叫杰克逊·布莱克。我过去没有见过你呀。

13. What do you do there?

你在那做什么工作？

14. I've been with IBM for years. I'm Mr. Field's Personal Assistant.

我已经在 IBM 工作好几年了。我是菲尔德先生的个人助理。

Tips：

In English-speaking cultures，people prefer shaking hands when they greet each other at the first time. There is usually a difference between "meet" for a first meeting and "see" for a second and subsequent meeting, e. g. "Nice to meet you" （first time），"Glad to see you （again）" （subsequent time）.

在讲英语的国家中，人们初次见面时喜欢使用握手的方式向对方表示问候。一般情况下，双方初次见面，用 "meet"，如 "Nice to meet you"；双方以后再见面应该用 "see"，如 "Glad to see you （again）"。

Dialogue 2   Meeting with the Manager

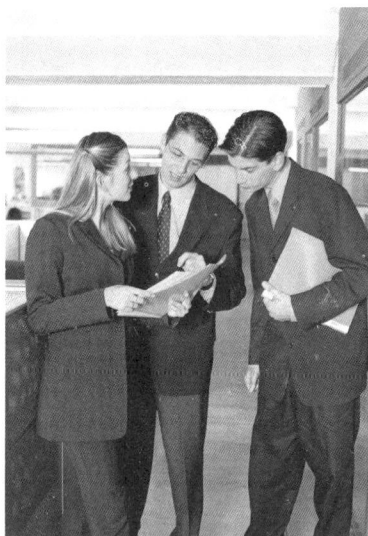

（K = Kary，the new staff of the company；L = Miss Lin，the manager of the Personnel Department；M = Mr. Martin，the manager of the Sales Department ）

L：Kary, I think I should show you around and let you meet all the staff① you'll be working with. Let's start from your boss, Johnson Martin.

K：Yes, thanks.

（in Mr. Martin's office）

L：She is the new staff, Kary.

M：Nice to meet you，Kary.

---

① staff 全体职员

K：Nice to meet you, Mr. Martin.

M：At first, welcome warmly for you to be one of our members. I hope you can be happy working here with us. I have to emphasize① that our employees are very capable with team spirit and creativity②. That's why our department is developing fast.

K：I am keen to share the same feeling. I believe I can also enjoy working here.

M：That's great. I'll show you the job description③. You'd better have a look at it first.

K：All right. Thank you.

M：Do you have any questions?

K：Not now. If I have any questions later, I will consult④ my colleagues or you.

M：OK. Nice seeing you here, Kary.

K：Nice seeing you here, too. I'm sorry to interrupt⑤ your today's work.

M：Of course not. Meeting you is the most important work for me today.

L：So, Kary, let me show you around the main departments.

K：Thanks a lot.

▶ Useful sentences

1. Kary, I think I should show you around and let you meet all the staff you'll be working with.

凯莉，我想我应该带你四周走走，认识一下要和你一起工作的员工们。

2. I have to emphasize that our employees are very capable with team spirit and creativity.

我得强调一下我们的雇员都很有团队精神和创造力。

3. I'll show you the job description.

我来给你看看工作职责说明。

4. If I have any questions later, I will consult my colleagues or you.

如果我以后有什么问题，我会和同事还有您商量的。

▶ Other useful sentences

1. I'm delighted⑥ to be working here.

我很高兴能来这里上班。

---

① emphasize 强调，着重

② creativity 创造性，创造力

③ description 描述，形容

④ consult 商议，商量

⑤ interrupt 打断（别人的话等），阻止

⑥ delighted 高兴的，欣喜的

2.　Let me introduce our General Manager，Mr. Robinson.

我来介绍一下我们的总经理，罗宾逊先生。

3.　Do you have any questions about your responsibility?

对于你的工作职责还有什么疑问吗？

4.　He is the After Sale Service Director.

他是售后服务部主任。

5.　Could you introduce me to the new Assistant Manager?

您能介绍我认识一下新来的经理助理吗？

6.　Paul is our accountant①.

保罗是我们的会计。

7.　Cathy will be our manager from now on.

从今天起凯瑟就是我们的经理了。

8.　Have we been introduced?

已经介绍过我们了吗？

9.　May I introduce myself?

我来介绍一下自己吧。

10.　Let me introduce you two.　This is Jack and this is Mary.

我来介绍一下你们两个。这位是杰克，这位是玛丽。

Tips：

Introductions and greetings in all languages have the same purpose：to establish contact with another person，to recognize his or her existence，and to show friendliness. There are two types of introductions：introducing yourself；introducing someone else and also there are two types of greetings：formal greetings；informal greetings. If you want to introduce someone else to others，first you have to let others know whom you are. If you want to show your friendliness and politeness to someone who you meet at the first time， you'd better use some formal greetings.

以任何一种语言所做的介绍与问候都有一个共同的目的：与他人建立关系、意识到他人的存在、表现出自己友好的一面。介绍主要分为两种：自我介绍、介绍他人。同时，问候也分为两种：正式问候、非正式问候。如果你想介绍两个素不相识的人认识，首先你要让他们认识你自己。如果你想给初次见面的人留下彬彬有礼的印象，那最好使用正式的问候用语。

———————————

①　accountant 会计人员，会计师

Dialogue 3   Introducing Kary to Colleagues in the Department

(K = Kary, the new staff of the company; L1 = Miss Lin, the manager of the Personnel Department; P = Paul, the colleague of Kary; E = Emily, the colleague of Kary; J1 = Jerry, the colleague of Kary; L2 = Linda, the colleague of Kary; J2 = Jack, the colleague of Kary)

L1: Now I'd like you to know all of our main departments. He is Paul and the manager of the Sales Department.

K : How do you do?

P : How do you do and welcome to be one of our members.

L1: She is the manager of the Research① and Development Department②.

E : Call me Emily. Nice to meet you.

K : Nice to meet you, too.

L1: And follow me, please. I'll show you the manager of the Production③ Department. Jerry, she is Kary, our new colleague.

J1: I hope you will be happy here.

K : I will. Shall I meet my team members?

L1: Sure, come with me. Linda, I would like you to meet our new comer. She is Kary, she just graduated from Guangdong Foreign Trade School.

L2: Nice to meet you.

———————————

① research 研究，追究

② department 部门，部

③ production 生产，制作

K ： Nice to meet you, too. I am new here and would appreciate① your guidance②.

L2： That's all right. I will try my best to help you with your work if you need.

K ： That's very kind of you.

J2： I am Jack. Welcome aboard③. Your desk is over there.

K ： Thanks.

▶ Useful sentences

1. Now I'd like you to know all of our main departments.

现在我想让你了解一下主要的部门。

2. I am new here and would appreciate your guidance.

我刚来这，请多多指教。

3. Welcome aboard.

欢迎你来本公司工作。

▶ Other useful sentences

1. Please guide Joanna to her office desk.

请带乔安娜去她的办公桌那。

2. It's a pleasure to meet you.

很荣幸见到你。

3. I will try my best to assist if you need any help.

如果需要帮忙，我会尽力的。

4. What department are you in?

你在哪个部门?

5. What position do you hold?

你担任什么职务?

6. What are you in charge of?

你负责什么?

7. What are you responsible for in the company?

你在公司的职责是什么?

8. I'm in charge of the personnel④ and training.

我负责人事以及培训。

---

① appreciate 感激，欣赏

② guidance 指导，引导

③ welcome aboard 欢迎加入

④ personnel 人事部门

9. I'm the secretary in the Purchasing① Department.

我是采购部的秘书。

10. Let me introduce Mr. Jackson to you.

我来给你介绍一下杰克逊先生。

11. Allow me to introduce Mr. Norton to you.

请允许我介绍诺顿先生给你认识。

12. I'd like to introduce Peter to you.

我想介绍彼得给你认识一下。

13. I'd like you to meet my friend Edward.

我想你认识一下我的朋友爱德华。

14. Meet my friend Edward, please?

来认识一下我的朋友爱德华。

15. Let me introduce my friend to you.

我来介绍我的朋友给你认识。

16. Who is the lady in white?

那位穿白衣服的女士是谁?

Tips:

If people in the office tend to order take-away food for lunch, you can volunteer to help with the ordering. A positive approach to helping is especially important for interns. As well as ordering lunch, interns should be ready to take on trivial tasks, such as photocopying and data research. If people in the office dine in the canteen, it's wise to politely ask those who sit around you to dine with you. This makes the invitation sound natural.

如果办公室的同事午餐要叫外卖,你可以主动帮他们订餐。这种积极的方法对于实习生们来说尤为重要。除了订午餐之外,实习生们还应随时准备接手做一些诸如复印材料和数据分析之类的琐碎事情。如果办公室中有人去餐厅吃饭,那你最好礼貌地邀请坐在自己周围的同事一起吃午饭,这会使得邀请听上去很自然。

Listening Practice

Listen to the following conversation and complete the sentences.

A: Good morning, Helen Wright. I think ＿＿＿＿＿＿＿ who's who in the ＿＿＿＿＿＿＿

---

① purchasing 购买

24

company. You'll need to know who to go to when you want to contact a particular manager. Let's start right from the top. David Clinton is the Manager Director. His Personal Assistant is Ruth Rice. The company is divided into four departments: _____ , clear?

B: Yes.

A: Right. George Brown looks after Production, and _____ . George Lewis works as Personal Assistant in the Production Department. Then there are two secretaries. Is that clear?

B: Yes.

A: Now let's _____ . We've got Lisa Leslie here, and her title is Personnel Manager.

B: I see.

A: And Jane Williams works for Lisa Leslie as Personal Assistant. And then there are two secretaries in the department, clear?

B: Yes. Thank you.

A: As you know, I'm the Marketing Manager. And for the next five months you'll work as my Personal Assistant. Judy Miller and Becky Parker, _____ . Then finally, Ray Allen is _____ . His PA is Cartier Martin. There are three secretaries in the department. I think you met them yesterday, right?

B: Yes.

Culture Note

1. Introduction is an important means in making strange people acquainted with each other in social intercourse. It can shorten the distance between people, step up understanding of each other and help expanding their social contact circle. On some formal occasions, it should be noted that the host or hostess is always introduced to the guests: the young to the old; men to women; employees to their bosses; unmarried women to the married; persons close to you to strangers, and later comers to early ones. With regard to people of the same generation or those you can not draw a clear distinction between their ages or status, there is a wide margin of free introductions.

2. Introducing one person to a group is difficult, which needs to be handled with tact. At a large gathering, you may either introduce a new comer to all the attendants one by one in sequence of their seats, or let an acquaintance help you to do so.

Pair Work

1. **Translate the following Chinese into English and do the role-play according to the dialogues.**

Dialogue 1：

A：我想你来认识一下玛丽，我们公司的新同事。

B：很高兴认识你，我想我们将一起工作。

A：是的。她将和你一起密切合作。你能带她到周围看看吗？

B：当然可以，请随我来。

Dialogue 2：

A：嗨，我的名字叫阿尔伯特。

B：你是新来这儿的，对吗？

A：是，我几天前刚开始工作。

B：欢迎来我们公司，如果有什么我可以为你做的，请告知。

A：谢谢，非常感激你。

Dialogue 3：

A：欢迎来我们公司。

B：谢谢，我很高兴来这工作。我能见见我的同事们吗？

A：当然可以，跟我来。玛丽，我想你认识一下我们的新同事，杰瑞。他刚毕业于广州大学。

C：很高兴认识你。

B：我新来到这个工作环境，请多多指教。

C：嗯，如果你需要任何帮助，我都会尽力帮忙的。

A：由于其他同事都不在这，我以后再把你介绍给他们吧。

B：好的。

Dialogue 4：

B：本，这是安吉拉，你的新同事。

C：嗨，安吉拉，欢迎来我们公司。

A：我很高兴能和你一起工作。

C：我也是。

B：好，现在让我们去二楼。我们可以搭电梯去那儿，那样会很快。这是爱德华，我们的会计；保罗，我们的出纳；麦格，我的秘书。这位是安吉拉，我们的新员工。

D：欢迎来到我们团队。

A：我很开心能来到这儿。

2. Imitate the above short dialogues and make new dialogues according to the following situations.

a. Suppose you are the secretary of the General Manager. Make an introduction of your colleagues to the new staff.

b. Suppose you are the department manager. Introduce the new comer to your team members.

Socializing Practice

▶ Role-play

A new employee will report to the company. Work with your partner deciding which role to play—the new employee or the office manager. Read your role card first and prepare for your words before you start.

Student A:

You are Cathy, the new employee of the Changlong International Company Limited. You are asked to report to the Human Resources Department. Your job is to meet the Human Resources Manager Mr. Zhang and have some idea of your jobs in detail. Cover the following main ideas:

- Meet the secretary of the department
- Meet the manager Mr. Zhang
- Know the detailed tasks
- Meet other colleagues

Student B:

You are the Human Resources Manager at Changlong International Company Limited. Your job is to receive the new staff, Cathy. Prepare for your dialogues according to the following points:

- Introduce the secretary, Joanna

- Greeting the new staff
- Make a brief introduction of her detailed tasks
- Show her to other colleagues

Daily Practice

▶ Tongue twister

1. Green glass globes glow greenly.

绿色玻璃球熠熠闪光。

2. Knife and a fork, bottle and a cork: that is the way you spell New York.

刀子和叉子，瓶子和木塞，这是你拼写纽约的方法。

3. A big black bug bit the big black bear, but the big black bear bit the big black bug back!

一只大黑臭虫咬大黑熊，大黑熊反过来咬了那只大黑臭虫！

4. Sheep shouldn't sleep in a shack; sheep should sleep in a shed.

羊儿不应住简棚，羊儿应住好羊棚。

5. I bought a bit of baking powder and baked a batch of biscuits. I brought a big basket of biscuits back to the bakery and baked a basket of big biscuits. Then I took the big basket of biscuits and the basket of big biscuits and mixed the big biscuits with the basket of biscuits that was next to the big basket and put a bunch of biscuits from the basket into a biscuit mixer and brought the basket of biscuits and the box of mixed biscuits and the biscuit mixer to the bakery and opened a tin of sardines.

我买了一点发酵粉，烤了一炉饼干。我带了一大篮子的饼干到面包店，烤了一篮子大饼干。然后我拿出一大篮子饼干和一篮子大饼干，把一大篮子里的饼干和大篮子旁边的篮子里的大饼干混合在一起，把这一堆饼干从篮子里放进饼干搅拌器，然后把一篮子饼干、一盒什锦饼干和饼干搅拌器拿到面包房，打开了一罐沙丁鱼。

▶ Read aloud

Youth is not a time of life; it is a state of mind; it is not a matter of rosy cheeks, red lips and supple knees; it is a matter of the will, a quality of the imagination, a vigor of the emotions; it is the freshness of the deep springs of life.

Youth means a temperamental predominance of courage over timidity, of the appetite for adventure over the love of ease that often exists in a man of 60 more than a boy of 20. Nobody grows old merely by a number of years. We grow old by deserting our ideals.

Years may wrinkle the skin, but to give up enthusiasm wrinkles the soul. Worry, fear, self-distrust bows the heart and turns the spirit back to dust.

Whether 60 or 16, there is in every human being's heart the lure of wonders, the unfailing appetite for what's next and the joy of the game of living. In the center of your heart and my heart, there is a wireless station; so long as it receives messages of beauty, hope, courage and power from man and from the infinite, so long as you are young.

When your aerials are down, and your spirit is covered with snows of cynicism and the ice of pessimism, then you've grown old, even at 20; but as long as your aerials are up, to catch waves of optimism, there's hope you may die young at 80.

Unit 3
Making More Contacts with Strangers

Learning Objectives

Now this is the first month for Kary to work in the company, and one day Kary is sent to meet a foreign guest at the airport. On another hand, Kary rents a house near the company in order to be convenient to go to work, and one day she meets a foreign neighbor at the housing estate. In this unit Kary needs to master some basic words, expressions and useful sentences to talk with strangers, some skills and etiquette of small talks. In our daily life, we always meet some strangers, so it's very important to know some social skills when we talk with them. Casual conversations and informal icebreakers offer opportunities to build rapport, create a cohesive team, and increase the chances of success. Learning how to communicate with strangers can reduce your anxiety in social situations, boost your confidence, lead you to new friends, and more.

Warming-up

1. What topics do you usually talk about with your friends?

2. Think of three questions you might ask a stranger when meeting for the first time. And think about what questions you should not ask when talking with a stranger.

3. What's the Chinese meaning for "small talk"? What shall we do before making a good small talk?

4. What gestures shall we pay attention to when we talk to a person?

Kary's Story

Dialogue 1   Meeting a Foreign Guest at the Airport

(K = Kary; G = Mr. Green, a businessman from Denmark. Kary holds a large sign reading "Welcome Mr. Green" at the airport, and Mr. Green comes up.)

K: Excuse me, are you Mr. Green from Denmark?

G：Yes, I am.

K：I'm Kary from ABC Company. My company sends me to meet you here.

G：Nice to meet you！

K：Nice to meet you, too, Mr. Green！ Welcome to China.

G：Thank you！

K：What about your trip on plane?

G：Nice. The service on board was superb①.

K：I'm glad to hear that. Oh, let me help you with your luggage②.

G：Thank you.

K：Is this your first visit to China?

G：Yes, and I hope it won't be my last.

K：I hope you will enjoy your stay in Guangzhou.

G：Thanks. I'm sure I will.

K：What do you think about the weather here?

G：Oh, it's fine. Warm and bright.

K：The car is waiting over there. Let's drive to the hotel.

G：OK. Let's go.

▶ Useful sentences

1. I'm Kary from … My company sends me to meet you here.

我是来自××公司的 Kary，我的公司派我来这里接你。

2. Oh, let me help you with your luggage.

让我帮你拿行李吧。

3. I hope you will enjoy your stay in Guangzhou.

祝愿你在广州过得愉快。

▶ Other useful sentences

1. Asking for name/identification of the visitor 询问来访者的姓名或身份

Are you Mr. Smith from ABC Company?

你是来自 ABC 公司的史密斯先生吗?

May I have your name, please?

请问您的名字?

2. Expressing regret when someone is not present 对被访者不在表示遗憾

I'm sorry, but Mr. Thomson has gone out to attend a conference.

---

① superb 极好的

② luggage 行李

很抱歉，汤姆斯先生外出参加一个会议了。

I'm sorry that the Marketing Manager is away on business.

很抱歉，市场营销部的经理出差去了。

3. Taking guests to their hotel 带领客人去宾馆

We've booked a western-style room for you, and I'll show you to your hotel.

我们已经为您订了一间西式房间，我将带您去宾馆。

You must be very tired after such a long trip.

经过这么长的旅途您一定很累吧。

Are you hungry? Would you like something to eat?

您饿了吗？要不要吃点东西？

4. Show the visitor around the company 带领来访者参观公司

This is our Sales Department.

这是我们的销售部。

I will show you our Production Department.

我会带您参观我们的生产部门。

Please allow me to show you our showroom.

请允许我带您参观我们的展览室。

5. Offer some help 提供帮助

I'm sorry, but our manager is not here. May I take your message?

很抱歉，我们经理不在。我可以帮您留言吗？

I'm sorry. Mr. Li is now in a meeting. Could you please call again in half an hour?

很抱歉，李先生正在开会。您能否在半小时后打来？

Wait a moment, please. I'll put you through to Mr. Zhang, our Export Manager.

请稍等。我将为您接通我们的出口部经理张先生。

6. Ask for some help 请求帮助

I'd like to speak to Mr. Davis. Would you get him on the phone, please?

我想找戴维斯先生。能否为我接通他的电话？

Please let me know your fax number. I'm sending a document.

请告诉我您的传真号，我要传一份文件。

Hello. This is Allen Snider. I'd like to know your e-mail address.

您好，我是斯奈德·艾伦，我想问一下你们的邮箱地址。

Tips:

How to Make Small Talk

1. Keep up with current events. Make small talk about the news, sports, your community and so on.

2. Comment on a piece of clothing or accessory. Ask where it came from, what the significance is, how much it cost. Making small talk is about being observant about people you don't know well.

3. Pay attention to what they're saying. When you're making small talk, follow up on phrases; for instance, if they say they're "excellent", ask why—ask where you can get some. If they mention that they're exhausted, follow up on it. When you're making small talk, remember that great conversations and good connections can be just around the corner.

4. Share an anecdote about your day. Did you lose your keys or find $10? Maybe you ate at a new restaurant recently, or found a great new CD. Making small talk is about sharing the little things.

5. Ask what movies or books they've seen or read recently. Someone once asked me that at a party. Admittedly, at first it felt contrived, but then we had a fantastic conversation about the book I was reading! Making small talk is about trying new conversations.

6. Talk about TV. Share your favorite TV shows. If you're Canadian, Little Mosque on the Prairie might be interesting to discuss! Making small talk about pop culture is easy and fun.

7. Recall your past conversations with the same person. Ask if their son is still ill or how the Mexican holiday went. Making small talk is easier when your memory is good.

8. Ask open-ended questions that require an explanation. For instance, "How are you?" isn't as effective as "Whatever happened with '_____' you were dealing with?"   ('_____' could be a business deal, family problem, or financial investment.) Remember that anything is a potential topic of conversation. You can even talk about how uncomfortable you are making small talk, and ask them how they do it.

Dialogue 2   Meeting a Foreign Friend at the Residence

(K = Kary; B = Bob Black, a businessman from the USA. One morning Kary and Mr. Black meet at the garden they live.)

K：Hi，good morning！

B：Good morning！Nice to meet you！

K：Nice to meet you，too！My name is Kary.

B：I am Bob Black．It's a lovely day，isn't it?

K：Wonderful sunshine！Do you live in this garden?

B：Yes．I've been living here for one year．Are you new here?

K：I moved in just last month，since I found a job near here.

M：Oh，that's great．It must be convenient① for you to go to work.

K：Right．It takes about 20 minutes to take a bus.

B：Good．And the surroundings② of this garden is quite nice，isn't it?

K：Terrific！A lot of plants，clean roads，and responsible security staff③．I am sure I've got a right place to live in.

B：Well said！I love here too.

K：Are you here for business?

B：Yes．My company sends me to China，and I also work nearby.

K：Good！Well，it's time for me to go to work．Hope to see you again.

B：Me too．Bye！

K：Bye！

▶▶ Useful sentences

1. It's a lovely day，isn't it?

天气很好，是吗?

2. And the surroundings of this garden is quite nice，isn't it?

这个花园的环境挺好的，是吗?

3. Well，it's time for me to go to work．Hope to see you again.

哦，我是时候去上班了。希望下次再见!

▶▶ Other useful sentences

1. Talking about the weather 谈论天气

Beautiful day，isn't it?

天气很好，是吗?

It looks like it's going to rain.

看起来快要下雨了。

---

① convenient 方便的

② surrounding（周围的）环境

③ security staff 保安

It's sunny/cloudy/windy/rainy/foggy/snowy.

天气晴朗/多云/有风/下雨/有雾/下雪。

2．At the office 在办公室

Looking forward to the weekend！

真期待周末！

Have you worked here long？

你在这里工作很久了吗？

Has it been a long week？

这是不是很漫长的一周啊？

You look like you need a cup of coffee.

你看起来需要一杯咖啡。

3．At a social event 在社交场合

Did you enjoy yourself？

玩得开心吗？

It looks like you could have another drink.

看起来你还可以再喝一杯哦。

Pretty nice place，huh？

这个地方不错，是吗？

I love your dress. Can I ask where you got it？

我很喜欢你的连衣裙。请问你是在哪里买的？

You look so great！

你看起来精神奕奕！

4．Leisure time and hobbies 娱乐与兴趣

Who is your favorite singer？

你最喜欢的歌星是谁？

What do you like to do with friends in your spare time？

你空闲时间喜欢和朋友做些什么？

How long have you been playing golf？

你打高尔夫球多久了？

Do you have any plans for Winter Break？

你冬天的假期有什么安排？

5．Talking about current news 讨论当前的新闻

Did you catch the news today？

你看今天的新闻了吗？

Did you hear about the fire on Wuyi Road？

你听说在五一路发生的火灾了吗？

What do you think about the earthquake?

你对这次地震怎么看？

Do you think Li Na is gonna win tonight?

你觉得李娜今晚会赢吗？

I heard that they were finally going to start building a new bridge.

我听说他们最后打算修建一座桥梁。

Dialogue 3　Meeting a Foreign Friend on a Business Trip

(K = Kary；S = Mr. Smith，a businessman from Canada. Kary is on a business trip to Shenzhen and now she is waiting to check in at a hotel. Mr. Smith is coming up to wait behind her.)

K：How do you do?

S：How do you do? So many people to stay at this hotel，right?

K：Yes. But it really enjoys a good reputation for its super service and comfortable facilities①. Are you a tourist?

S：No, I came on a business trip to inspect a factory here to see if there is the possibility of starting a joint venture② here.

K：So wonderful！May I know what products you handle③，please?

S：Electronic products.

K：Oh, I think you come to the right place. Shenzhen is well-known for its various and modern electronic products in China，and even in the world.

S：Yes，it's an amazing④ city. Do you come here to travel?

K：No. I'm here to attend a training course.

S：That's great！May I have your name，please?

K：My name is Kary，the secretary in ABC Company. And you?

S：My name is John Smith，Production Manager of Future Electronic Products in Canada.

K：Mr. Smith，nice talking with you.

S：The same to me，Kary.

---

① facilities 设备，设施
② a joint venture 合资企业
③ handle 经营
④ amazing 令人惊异的

▶ Useful sentences

1. But it really enjoys a good reputation for its super service and comfortable facilities.

但它确实因为优良的服务和舒适的设施而享有盛名。

2. I came on a business trip to inspect a factory here to see if there is the possibility of starting a joint venture here.

我此行出差是来调研一家工厂以看看是否有机会开展合资企业。

3. May I know what products you handle, please?

我是否能问一下你们经营的是什么产品?

4. Shenzhen is well-known for its various and modern electronic products in China, and even in the world.

深圳有各种现代化的电子产品,在中国甚至全世界都很出名。

Listening Practice

Listen to the recording and select the correct answer for each sentence, which may be missing one or more words.

1. What's your _____?
A. I'm Nancy.　　　　B. I'm from Russia.　　　　C. I'm a student.

2. Where do you _____?
A. I'm from Canada.　　　B. I live in Chicago.　　　C. I'm fine.

3. How's _____?
A. Okay.　　　　　B. I'm going to school.　　　　C. No problem.

4. _____ does she _____?
A. She likes to work.
B. She's a teacher.
C. She works at City Bank.

5. _____ they _____?
A. They're from Mexico.　B. They are in school.　　C. They live in Tokyo.

6. _____?
A. I'm getting married soon.
B. My father is a doctor.
C. I have three brothers.

7. _____?
A. I'm fine.　　　　B. Nothing much.　　　　C. That's too bad.

8. _____?
A. He's Japanese.　　　B. He's from Italy.　　　C. He's an engineer.

9. _____?

A. I like to exercise.　　B. I'm busy this weekend.　　C. I don't like sports.

10. _____?

A. He lives in Hong Kong.　B. He works downtown.　　C. He's a doctor.

Culture Note

How to Talk to Strangers

1. Let go of your ego

Prepare to be ignored. Prepare to be brushed off in a dramatic fashion. But also prepare to meet (and possibly date) people of unique charm and beauty. When you take the risk of talking to someone you don't know, rejection is certainly a possibility. So when you're out and about, leave the ego behind and keep the following in mind:

(1) Try to see failure as exciting—it's a chance to learn and improve.

(2) People don't bite. A lot of people are really open to conversation. In fact, you'd be amazed at how many people will be practically overjoyed that you come and talk to them, as if they've been waiting for you to approach them.

(3) Rejection is no big deal. This can't be emphasized enough. Still, fear of rejection will be the main reason why people don't go out and try this. If you are willing to get rejected, brush it off and keep going. You will have an awesome life.

(4) The people around you aren't watching you approach strangers. And, even when they are, it's usually in shock and awe, rather than because they're laughing at you.

2. Know how to start a conversation with a stranger

Don't count on other people to come to you; be ready and willing to walk up to anyone who looks interesting and forge a connection. Make sure you know how to use confidence and welcoming body language to disarm anyone who might be on their guard.

3. Keep it simple

Don't come in with "canned material", "nuclear attraction" routines, or other social robotics. The best way to make a connection with someone is to come from the heart and live fully in the moment.

(5) What you say isn't nearly as important as how you say it. Socializing is about exchanging energy, not being a wordsmith.

(6) When in doubt, just say "Hi". If you've never done this before, you may get brushed off several, even dozens of times until you get really comfortable being yourself in front of other people.

(7) Try beginning with an experience that you and the stranger are both experiencing

together. Perhaps a baby is crying annoyingly in the room or you and the stranger are at the theater, walking out of a really bad movie. Use these shared experiences to create conversation starting questions or statements. Breaking the ice is easier when you can create a connection with the stranger. Also, they will likely already have an opinion on the matter to share in response.

4. Try often

If you're still terrified by the idea of talking to strangers, challenge yourself to talk to one stranger a day, every day, for 30 days. If you're walking past someone on the sidewalk, say "Hi", and the person looks at you and keeps walking (done that many times), your job is done for the day. If you walk up to a girl in a club and say "Hey", and she responds, with a slightly grossed out look "I have a boyfriend", congratulations — you're one step closer to improving your love life. The point of this exercise is to get you used to talking to people you don't know and form the habit of being more social.

Pair Work

1. **Discuss with your partner about the following topics, and then decide which are suitable topics and which are unsuitable topics when we talk with a stranger.**

   a. personal questions

   b. people's age and income

   c. the weather

   d. hire style

   e. religion and politics

   f. marriage situation

   g. jobs

   h. leisure interests

   i. sports news

   j. entertainment news

   k. clothes

   l. study

   Suitable Topics

   Unsuitable Topics

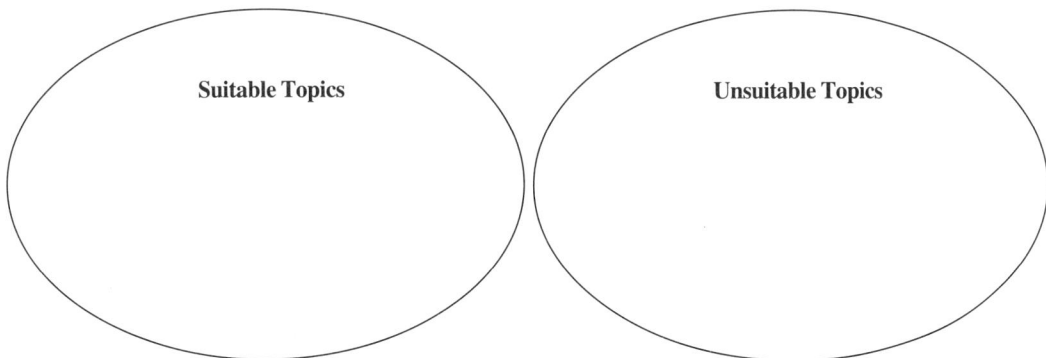

2. **Discuss with your partner about the following topics, and then decide what we can do and what we cannot do when we talk with a stranger.**

a. use encouraging noises and gestures

b. keep good eye contact

c. yawn

d. sigh

e. change the subject

f. ask for more information to show your interest

g. look away from the person who's talking to you

h. use positive body language

i. look at your watch

j. finish other people's sentences for them

Can	Can't

3. Complete the conversation with your partner.

(*Two new students in a college meet for the first time at the beginning of the first term.*)

A：Hello. May I help you with your luggage?

B：Thank you very much!

A：You are welcome. What's your name?

B：Helen. And yours?

A：Tom…

【Socializing Practice】

▶ Situational Practice 1

Use open-ended questions to ask your partner about the suitable topics in exercise 1 in pair work. And there are some samples for you.

● How do you …

● What/ Why/ When …

● What do you think of …

- Describe for me …
- Tell me about …

Situational Practice 2

Mr. Hunter, a Japanese businessman, comes for his appointment with Mr. Hansen. But Mr. Hansen is at the meeting. You are the assistant to Mr. Hansen, and you receive Mr. Hunter. Now, you …

- ask for the basic information about the visitor.
- explain the situation.
- offer some tea and magazines.

Situational Practice 3

This week the school's English Salon invites some foreign students from other schools. You attend the Salon and meet a foreign friend. Try to talk with him and make friends with him. You can refer to the following steps:

1. Make greetings.
2. Introduce yourself.
3. Ask some information about the foreign student, such as the school name, major, interests and so on.
4. Talk something about yourself, such as the major, interests, your school life and so on.

Daily Practice

Tongue twister

1. A box of biscuits, a batch of mixed biscuits.

一盒饼干，一炉什锦饼干。

2. Betty and Bob brought back blue balloons from the big bazaar.

贝蒂和鲍勃在大型的义卖市场买了蓝气球回来。

3. A pleasant place to place a plaice is a place where a plaice is pleased to be placed.

放置鲽最好的地方是鲽愿意被放置的地方。

4. A tutor who tooted a flute tried to tutor two tooters to toot. Said the two to their tutor, "Is it harder to toot or to tutor two tooters to toot?"

一个吹笛的导师尝试教两个吹笛者吹笛。那两个学吹笛的问导师："吹笛难，还是教两个学吹笛的人吹笛难呢？"

5. A bitter biting bittern bit a better brother bittern, and the bitter better bittern bit the bitter biter back. And the bitter bittern, bitten, by the better bitten bittern, said: "I'm a bitter biter bit, alack!"

一只沮丧而尖刻的麻鸦咬了它兄弟一口，而没有它那么沮丧的兄弟又咬它一口。那只被咬的沮丧麻鸦对它的兄弟说："我是一只充满怨恨的麻鸦！我害人终害己了！"

▶ Read aloud

Work and Pleasure

To be really happy and really safe, one ought to have at least two or three hobbies, and they must all be real. It is no use starting late in life to say: "I will take an interest in this or that." Such an attempt only aggravates the strain of mental effort. A man may acquire great knowledge of topics unconnected with his daily work, and yet hardly get any benefit or relief. It is no use doing what you like; you have got to like what you do. Broadly speaking, human being may be divided into three classes: those who are toiled to death, those who are worried to death, and those who are bored to death. It is no use offering the manual laborer, tired out with a hard week's sweat and effort, the chance of playing a game of football or baseball on Saturday afternoon. It is no use inviting the politician or the professional or business man, who has been working or worrying about serious things for six days, to work or worry about trifling things at the weekend.

It may also be said that rational, industrious, useful human beings are divided into two classes: first, those whose work is work and whose pleasure is pleasure; and secondly, those whose work and pleasure are one. Of these the former are the majority. They have their compensations. The long hours in the office or the factory bring with them as their reward, not only the means of sustenance, but a keen appetite for pleasure even in its simplest and most modest forms. But Fortune's favored children belong to the second class. Their life is a natural harmony. For them the working hours are never long enough. Each day is a holiday, and ordinary holidays when they come are grudged as enforced interruptions in an absorbing vacation. Yet to both classes the need of an alternative outlook, of a change of atmosphere, of a diversion of effort, is essential. Indeed, it may well be that those whose work is their pleasure are those who most need the means of banishing it at intervals from their minds.

Unit 4   Communicating with Colleagues

Learning Objectives

Kary is going to work in a new company. Kary's objectives are to show us how to introduce jobs and responsibilities to a new staff, help other colleagues and praise the employees. Kary's experience will show us that for a new colleague he or she should know the basic rules of the company first, volunteer to lend a hand to someone else and get a praise if he or she works hard.

Warming-up

1. For a new staff, how can he or she start the new work smoothly?
   a. How can he/she try to be familiar with other colleagues?
   b. How can he/she try to be familiar with the personnel?
   c. How can he/she master the basic rules of the company?
2. If you are a new employee, how can you get the positive attitude from the boss and other colleagues? Choose the answer and tell the reasons.
   a. Your work.
   b. Your attitude to other colleagues.
   c. Your daily life after work.

Kary's Story

Dialogue 1   Knowing the Routine and Details of the Work

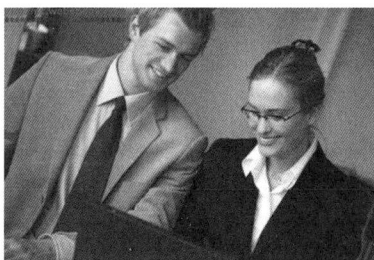

（K = Kary，the new staff of the company；L = Linda，the colleague of Kary）

K：Linda，could you tell me when our work starts?

L：Yes. We should get to work before nine in the morning. We can have an hour break for the lunch and have a rest at noon. And leave our company after five thirty in the afternoon.

K：Thanks. Shall we wear the uniform① when we are in the company?

L：Yes. When you are in the company，you must wear it.

K：Shall I make up everyday?

L：You'd better do. That will make you look really good. But pay attention，you cannot make up heavily.

K：I will. Thanks.

L：Have you prepared for your work schedule②? I hope you have known the requirements of your routine③ work.

K：Yes，of course. I know it is the most important thing. Would you like to show me how to operate the office equipments? It looks complicated④.

L：It's easy to use. The directions here show you how to make bulk⑤ copies and two-sided copies. These are the slide projector，notebook computers and the small TV. You can borrow these equipments for presentations⑥. This is the fax machine.

K：I have known how to use all of the machines. How convenient! Thanks for your help.

▶ Useful sentences

1. Shall we wear the uniform when we are in the company?

我们在公司时必须穿制服吗?

2. But pay attention，you cannot make up heavily.

但是请注意，你不能化浓妆。

3. Would you like to show me how to operate the office equipments?

请你给我演示一下怎样操作这些办公设备好吗?

4. You can borrow these equipments for presentations.

你可以借这些设备来陈述。

---

① uniform 制服，军服

② schedule 进度表，时刻表

③ routine 日常工作，例行公事

④ complicated 结构复杂的，麻烦的

⑤ bulk 大批的，大量的

⑥ presentation 陈述，报告

▶ Other useful sentences

1. Inquiring about the rules of the company 询问公司规定

Excuse me, sir. Could you tell me when the work starts?

打扰了，先生。你能告诉我什么时候开始上班吗？

Can we have a break at noon?

我们中午的时候有休息吗？

If I were late for the work, what's the punishment[①]?

如果我迟到了，有什么惩罚吗？

Is there any requirement for our clothes?

对衣服有要求吗？

2. Showing thanks to your colleagues 对同事表示感谢

Are you sure you don't mind?

这样会不会太麻烦您了？

That would be a great help.

那可帮了我大忙。

3. Talking about the relationship of your colleagues 谈论同事关系

I am on good terms with my colleagues.

我和我的同事相处得很好。

I am compatible[②] with my partner.

我和我的搭档很合得来。

We co-operated well together the work down.

我们同心协力把工作做完了。

I have some problems working together with her.

我和她在工作中存在一些问题。

She always gives me the cold shoulder.

她总是不搭理我。

He always takes the credit for the work we've done together.

他总是把我们共同工作的功劳占为己有。

I don't like anybody who flatters[③] me.

我不喜欢对我溜须拍马的人。

He isn't really sociable[④].

---

① punishment 惩罚

② compatible 相容的，和谐的

③ flatter 奉承，阿谀

④ sociable 好交际的

他不太善于交际。

Maybe you should communicate with him like a friend.

也许你应该像朋友那样跟他交流。

Tips：

Even the smallest courtesies kindle a fire that ignites chemistry and builds kinship. The courtesy of saying "hello" when you come into the office after being away. The courtesy of letting people know when you're going to be away for an extended period. The courtesy of honoring policies about reserving rooms, spaces, and equipment for activities. The courtesy of a simple "please", "thank you" and "you're welcome" for small favors.

即便最小的礼貌也会激发融洽感，点燃亲密的"火焰"。比如回到办公室时说声"嗨"；不能按时赶回来时，要和别人说一声；遵守为活动预留房间、空间、设备的规定；对帮助给予一个简单的"请""谢谢""不客气"。

Dialogue 2   Apologizing for the Mistake at Work

(K = Kary，the new staff of the company；L = Linda，the colleague of Kary，helping Kary to be familiar with the new work)

L：Kary，did you make out this form?

K：Yes，I did. Is there anything wrong with it?

L：You have made mistakes with not only the client's name but also the figures. It's not funny，Kary. If I had not noticed it，we could have lost a lot of money.

K：Oh，I am rather careless. I am really sorry for my mistakes. I feel so bad and hope that you can accept my apology①. And I promise it won't happen again.

L：I think I shouldn't shout at you. I am too serious. It is all right. Don't keep it in mind. When I was new in the company，I had also made the similar mistakes.

K：What can I do for you to make up?

L：I don't think you need. I have forgiven you. You don't really mean that，do you? I shouldn't give you so much pressure②.

K：You're a good friend to me. Thank you so much.

---

① apology 道歉，认错

② pressure 压（力）

▶ Useful sentences

1. Did you make out this form?

是你制的这张表格吗?

2. I feel so bad and hope that you can accept my apology.

我感觉很糟糕，希望你能接受我的道歉。

3. What can I do for you to make up?

我能为你做些什么来弥补呢?

4. I shouldn't give you so much pressure.

我不应该给你那么大的压力。

▶ Other useful sentences

1. Showing your apology 表示道歉

I must apologize① for what I said.

我必须对我说的话表示歉意。

I feel really bad about that.

我对那件事真的感到非常抱歉。

Please forgive me. I really didn't mean that.

请原谅。我真的不是那个意思。

How could I be so thoughtless?

我怎么会那么粗心大意呢?

How can I make it up to you?

我要怎样才能补偿你?

It's all my fault.

全是我的错。

Will you ever forgive me?

你会原谅我吗?

I'm sorry for giving you so much trouble.

对不起，给你添了这么多麻烦。

2. Comforting others 安慰别人

That's quite all right.

那真的没关系。

It doesn't matter at all.

一点没关系。

You're forgiven.

---

①   apologize 道歉，认错

我原谅你。

No problem. We all make mistakes.

没问题。人人都有犯错的时候。

It's not your fault.

那不是你的错。

Don't worry about it.

别放在心上。

Think no more of it.

别再想它了。

Don't give it another thought.

不要再想了。

Okay. I accept your apology.

好吧，我接受你的道歉。

Tips：

Day in and day out, it's the small things that kill our spirit: The sales rep who empties his cold coffee and leaves the splatters all over the sink. The manager who uses the last drop of lotion and doesn't refill the container. The analyst who walks away from the printer, leaving the red light flashing "paper jam". The boss who walks into the reserved conference room in the middle of a meeting and bumps everybody out for an "urgent" strategic planning meeting. The person who cuts in line at the cafeteria cash register. The guy who answers his cell phone and tries to carry on a conversation out loud in the middle of a meeting. Try to be courteous. Or you will leave a bad impression in other people's minds. And that will of course influence the relationship between you and others.

日复一日，让我们崩溃的都是小事情：销售代表将冷掉的咖啡倒入水池，溅得里边到处都是；经理用光最后一滴洗手液，却不重新把瓶子装满；分析员从打印机旁离开，却让它闪烁着红色"卡纸"灯；老板闯进正在开会的会议室，把大家都赶出来，为"紧急"战略规划会议腾出地方；有人在餐厅收银台插队；有人在会议中接手机，并大声讲电话。要注意礼貌，否则你就会给别人留下坏印象，那肯定会影响到你和他人的关系。

Dialogue 3   Work Communication

(K = Kary, the new staff of the company; L = Linda, the colleague of Kary who has been helping Kary to be familiar with her work)

L: Kary, time passes quickly. You have worked here for a month. How's your feeling?

K: I think I'm really busy. I am busy answering phones, typing and printing and writing reports and contacting customers.

L: I had the same feeling when I first came to work here. But after a period of time, I feel better. I am sure you'll get used to this busy job.

K: I also feel that the work efficiency① here is very high, and you have strong working ability and professional② skill. It seems that you know all. That's really wonderful!

L: You know the phrase: the survival③ of the fittest. We have no choices.

K: That's right. And now I enjoy my busy work. I find I can work better under pressure.

L: No wonder you have been familiar with all the business in our department. Well done.

K: It's very kind of you to say so, Linda. I shall work harder. I have much support from our team and especially you. Without you, I could not get the achievement④.

L: Don't keep it in mind. If you have any difficulty later, don't hesitate to turn to me for help. I will always be pleased to help you. We are good friends, aren't we?

K: Yes, of course we are. Thank you for saying so.

---

① efficiency 效率

② professional 专业的，专业性的

③ survival 幸存，生存

④ achievement 完成，达到

▶ Useful sentences

1. I also feel that the work efficiency here is very high.

我也感觉到这儿的工作效率非常高。

2. You have strong working ability and professional skill.

你有很强的工作能力和职业技能。

3. I find I can work better under pressure.

我发现在有压力的情况下能更出色地工作。

4. Without you, I could not get the achievement.

没有你，我不可能取得这个成绩。

▶ Other useful sentences

1. Describing the working situation 描述工作情况

Working in foreign enterprises① involves② busy schedules and great pressure.

在外企工作很忙，压力很大。

Our employees are very capable with team spirit and creativity.

我们的员工都很能干，具有团队精神和创造性。

I have a great team working with me.

我有一个很棒的团队与我一起工作。

2. Praising your colleague's excellent work 表扬你同事的出色工作

You really did a good job.

你工作干得不错。

Well, your time has been well spent.

你工作的效果非常明显。

Well done.

干得好。

I admire③ your work.

我很欣赏你的工作。

I respect your work.

我对你的工作表示敬意。

You are very professional.

你非常专业。

You are really talented④.

---

① enterprise 企（事）业单位，事业
② involve 包含，牵涉
③ admire 赞赏，称赞
④ talented 有才能的，有才干的

你很有天赋。

He is bouncy①.

他精力充沛。

I have heard so much of you.

久仰大名。

I get mind of you.

久仰大名。

3. Expressing thanks for other's praise（对别人的表扬表示感谢）

You flatter me.

您过奖了。

I shall work harder.

我应多努力才行。

Tips：

　　To be heard you have to make people like you. You need to create chemistry with your staff as a manager and need to create chemistry with your team, with your boss, with your customer, with your strategic partners as a project leader. People believe people they like. That's not a news bulletin. Great communicators develop the "likeability factor" — your personality and the "chemistry" you create between yourself and others.

　　想要别人听你说话，你得先让人家喜欢你。经理得和员工相处融洽；项目组长需要和队友、老板、顾客、战略伙伴合作默契。人们相信他们喜欢的人。这不是什么新闻。好的交流者能产生出"亲和力"——这来自你的个性和你制造的融洽感觉。

---

① bouncy 快活的，精神的

Listening Practice

Listen to the following conversation and complete the sentences.

(C = Colleague, B = Benjamin)

C: I can't stand that stupid guy any longer. He's unbelievable.

B: Oh, my dear lady, take it easy. You should _____ like him.

C: He does everything so mindlessly, he is going to drive me crazy.

B: I suggest you talk with him and teach him _____ problems properly.

C: I've told him how to do that several times, but he's never listened to me.

B: Maybe you _____ just like a friend, not a boss.

C: Oh, I always have difficulty in _____ the staff.

B: Just treat them as your good friends and talk with them as we do. Make sure you don't lose your temper!

C: Oh, that's tough. I'm afraid I'll have to change my image.

B: No, that's not necessary. Just _____ and their own _____.

C: But sometimes they offer some useless proposals, awfully useless.

B: Well, no one is perfect.

C: That's right. I should speak to them politely.

B: All men are equal in the eyes of the God. We are all equal _____ in the team.

C: Thanks very much. You're very eloquent[1].

B: Thanks for saying that.

---

[1] eloquent 雄辩的，有口才的

Culture Note

1.   Every office has its own protocol for who is called by his or her first name and who is called by his or her title. New employees should follow suit, after listening carefully to how people are addressed.

2.   Office protocol can make it different for one to ask another for help. Most people will volunteer to lend a hand to someone who has helped him or her. If you know a coworker is working through lunch to collate a large client packet, your volunteering to stay and help will be gratefully received and most often returned when it's you who is stuck. If your offer is accepted, you simply hope the favor will be returned when it's you who is overloaded.

3.   Praise is something which many bosses don't give enough of. When some of them do decide to praise, it somehow does not have the maximum desired impact on the employee. Recognition of good work is essential to drive your employees further. Praise is something that needs to be imparted correctly when it's due to the individual or team. So make sure the praise is authentic, specific, immediate and unstained.

Pair Work

1.   **Tony is the staff in Chang Hong Company Limited and he has some difficulty in running his new project. The following is the talk between Tony and the manager of Engineering Department. Your tasks are:**

   a.   Translate the following Chinese sentences into English.

   b.   Do the role-play according to the whole dialogue.

(M = Manager, T = Tony)

M: How is the project going?

T：Well，frankly speaking，I am running a little behind. It's 40% done.

经理：在工作过程中有什么困难吗？你应该加快进度了。

T：I have little chance to communicate with colleagues when I have problems. They are always too busy to help a green hand like me.

M：Have you ever helped others when they are in trouble? Most will give a hand to someone who has helped him.

托尼：我帮过。但是我很苦恼的是没人愿意帮我。

经理：你应该和其他同事很好地合作，你要知道科学的时间进度表能提高工作效率。

托尼：我明白你的意思，但是我似乎和他们合不来。

M：Cheer up and pay more attention to your colleagues and the things will be much better. I am speaking from my experience.

T：Thank you so much.

经理：你也应该多读书，丰富知识。

托尼：是个好主意。从书上能学到很多有用的东西。

M：We're approaching the critical point for success or failure of this project；you'd better speed up and catch up with others.

T：Well，I will do it better.

M：If you have any problem in your work，please let me know.

T：Thanks very much. I promise I will work harder.

2. Make dialogues according to the following situations.

a. Suppose you are the new employee of the AMG Company. Make a dialogue about the introduction of the detailed work and other requirements of your company.

b. Suppose you are the boss. Make a dialogue about praising your new staff because of his or her excellent job.

Socializing Practice

▶ Role-play

A new employee tries to be familiar with the rules and customs of the new company. Working with a partner，decide which role to take—the new employee or another staff. Read your role card first and prepare for your words before you start.

Student A：

You are Dora，the new employee of the VEGA Import and Export Corporation. You are asked to talk to Delia，your colleague. Your job is to learn something about the uniform and other rules of your company. Cover the following main ideas：

- meet Delia，one of the colleague of your department
- ask about the uniform and working time
- ask about the holidays
- ask about the other rules

Student B：

You are Delia，the old staff of the VEGA Import and Export Corporation. Your job is to introduce the rules and customs to your new colleague，Dora. Prepare for your dialogues according to the following points：

- meet Dora，the new colleague of your department
- introduce the rules of uniform and working time
- introduce the rules of holidays
- introduce and emphasize other rules of your company and department

Daily Practice

▶▶ Tongue twister

1. Can you can a can as a canner can can a can?

你能像用开罐器打开罐头一样，把一个罐头打开吗？

2. When you write copy you have the right to copyright the copy you write.

当你写好了稿子时，你就有权为这篇你写的稿子取得版权。

3. I have got a date at a quarter to eight；I'll see you at the gate，so don't be late.

我在八点差一刻有个约会，我会在大门口见你，所以别迟到。

4. Mary Mac's mother's making Mary Mac marry me. My mother's making me marry mary Mac. Will I always be so merry when Mary's taking care of me? Will I always be so merry when I marry Mary Mac?

玛丽·麦克的母亲把玛丽·麦克嫁给我；我的母亲让我娶玛丽·麦克；当玛丽照顾我的时候，我会总是觉得高兴吗？如果我娶了玛丽会一直快乐吗？

5. All I want is a proper cup of coffee made in a proper copper coffee pot. You can believe it or not，but I just want a cup of coffee in a proper copper coffee pot. Tin copper coffee pots or iron coffee pots are of no use to me. If I can't have a proper cup of coffee in a proper copper coffee pot，I'll have a cup of tea!

我只想要一杯用真正铜制的咖啡壶煮的正统咖啡。信不信由你，我只想要一杯用真正铜制的咖啡壶煮的正统咖啡。锡制的咖啡壶和铁制的咖啡壶对我而言也是没用的。假如我不能要一杯用真正铜制的咖啡壶煮的正统咖啡，那我就要一杯茶吧!

▶ Read aloud

Be Happy!

The days that make us happy make us wise.
—John Masefield

When I first read this line by England's Poet Laureate, it startled me. What did Masefield mean? Without thinking about it much, I had always assumed that the opposite was true. But his sober assurance was arresting. I could not forget it.

Finally, I seemed to grasp his meaning and realized that here was a profound observation. The wisdom that happiness makes possible lies in clear perception, not fogged by anxiety nor dimmed by despair and boredom, and without the blind spots caused by fear.

Active happiness—not mere satisfaction or contentment—often comes suddenly, like an April shower or the unfolding of a bud. Then you discover what kind of wisdom has accompanied it. The grass is greener; bird songs are sweeter; the shortcomings of your friends are more understandable and more forgivable. Happiness is like a pair of eyeglasses correcting your spiritual vision.

Nor are the insights of happiness limited to what is near around you. Unhappy, with your thoughts turned in upon your emotional woes, your vision is cut short as though by a wall. Happy, the wall crumbles.

The long vista is there for the seeing. The ground at your feet, the world about you—people, thoughts, emotions, pressures—are now fitted into the larger scene. Everything assumes a fairer proportion. And here is the beginning of wisdom.

Unit 5   Communicating with Customers

Learning Objectives

Kary's job in the company is Sales Assistant, so she should help her manager sell their products to overseas market. In this unit Kary tries to talk to their foreign customers by herself. She needs to introduce their products, negotiate the trade terms, promote the business and reply to customers' questions. She needs to grasp some effective communication skills and successful customer communication strategy. Running a business allows for a variety of opportunities to interact with your customers. It's important to take advantage of these opportunities to create repeat—and hopefully life-long—customer relationships. Miscommunication with customers often results in the loss of business. Communicating with your customers allows you to find out how they feel about what you provide and what they require from your business; it allows you to develop relationships with your top customers.

Warming-up

1. How to negotiate with customers more effectively?
2. If you can't meet a buyer's request, what'll you do?
3. Under what circumstances shall we change the negotiation style?

Kary's Story

Dialogue 1   Talking about the Price with a Customer

(K = Kary; E = Mr. Ellison, a new customer from Australia. Kary sent a sample to Mr. Ellison last week. Now Kary calls Mr. Ellison about the sample.)

K: Good afternoon. May I speak to Mr. Ellison?

E: Good afternoon. This is Mr. Ellison speaking. Who's that, please?

K: This is Kary from Guangdong ABC Imp & Exp Corporation.

E: Hi, Kary. How are you?

K: Fine. Thanks. I call to see whether you received the sample of the handbag we sent last week?

57

E：Oh, yes. We are quite interested in it. If the price is acceptable，we'll consider placing an order.

K：I am very glad to hear that.

E：What's your best price?

K：The unit price is $8.50 FOB Guangzhou.

E：I should say that this price is too high.

K：But Mr. Ellison, you can see from our sample that our products are made of quality material① with fine workmanship②. And this is the latest design with fashionable style. They sell well in a lot of market.

E：Well, I do not deny that. But since this is our first transaction, I hope you can give some discount.

K：Mr. Ellison, if you can purchase 5,000 pieces, we can consider giving you 5% discount.

E：But Kary, your brand is new to our market，and we can only place a trial order③ to see the market potential. I think 3,000 pieces would be more suitable.

K：How about this, 4% discount for 3,000 pieces. This is our bottom price④, and I offer it with a view to our future business.

E：OK, thank you, Kary. Please fax me your proforma invoice, and we'll send you an order later on.

K：No problem. I will fax it to you today. Keep in touch, goodbye！

E：Bye！

▶ Useful sentences

1. If the price is acceptable, we'll consider placing an order.

如果价格可以接受，我们会考虑下订单。

2. But Mr. Ellison, you can see from our sample that our products are made of quality material with fine workmanship.

埃利森先生，你可以从我们的样品看出，我们的产品是用上乘的材料和精湛的工艺做成的。

3. But Kary, your brand is new to our market, and we can only place a trial order to see the market potential.

但是凯莉，你们的品牌在我们的市场上是新的，因此我们只能下试订单以看看

---

① quality material 优良的材质

② fine workmanship 精湛的工艺

③ trial order 试订单

④ bottom price 最低价

市场的潜力。

4．How about this，4% discount for 3,000 pieces. This is our bottom price，and I offer it with a view to our future business.

要不这样吧，对于 3 000 件我们提供 4% 的折扣。这是我们的最低价，希望我们能保持长期合作。

▶▶ Other useful sentences

1．Starting the negotiation 开始洽谈

I suggest we start by the specification of the products. Is that acceptable to you?

我建议我们从产品的规格开始，你觉得可以吗？

Let's begin with the price，OK?

让我们从价格开始，好吗？

2．Explaining your interests 阐述意向

We are particularly interested in Model No. 126.

我们对 126 款特别感兴趣。

We are concerned about the functions of the product.

我们关心的是产品的功能。

3．Making suggestions 提出建议

We propose that a team of experts should investigate the problem.

我们建议要有一队专家调查这个问题。

I suggest you go over the brochure first.

我建议你先浏览一下这个小册子。

4．Making concessions 做出让步

If you order 5,000 pieces，then we will give you a ten percent discount.

如果你们订 5 000 件，那么我们将给你们提供 10% 的折扣。

If you could give us a long term contract，we would drop the price by 15%．

如果你们能与我方签订一个长期的合同，我们将降价 15%。

Provided that you can ship the goods immediately，this price is acceptable to us.

如果你们能立即发货，我们能接受这个价格。

5．Reaching settlement 达成协议

I think we can manage that.

我想我们能设法做到。

We have a deal then.

那么我们就达成协议了。

6．Ending the negotiation 结束洽谈

I'd like to thank you all for coming. I think it has been a really fruitful meeting.

感谢你们所有人的到来。我想这是一个很有成果的会议。

Thank you very much. I hope you'll have a good journey back.

非常感谢你们。祝愿你们回程时旅途愉快！

Tips：

Breakdown — Try to avoid breakdown but do not seek an agreement at all costs.

It is possible that you may not be able to reach agreement. For example, you might find that your interests are so far apart that agreement is not possible.

If it appears impossible to move any further, do not give up too easily. There are a number of things you can do.

1. Summarize what has been agreed so far. This will remind you of any positive result.

2. Try to ask new questions.

3. Remember your best alternative to negotiated agreement.

4. Keep calm. Do not show anger towards the other party.

5. Try to leave the door open for future meetings.

Dialogue 2　Talking about the Payment Terms and Shipment Date

(K = Kary; E = Mr. Ellison, the customer in Dialogue 1. Since Mr. Ellison has placed an order with Kary, now he calls Kary to talk about more details.)

E：Good morning, Kary!

K：Good morning, Mr. Ellison.

E：You received our order for the 3,000 pieces of handbags, right?

K：Yes, Mr. Ellison. Thank you very much!

E：Today I call to talk more about this order with you. What would be the payment terms①?

K：According to our usual practice②, we require payment by confirmed, irrevocable L/C available by draft at sight.

E：L/C would be no problem. But as for the confirmed one, it will be quite a lot of difficulty for us. You see, we need to put much deposit③ in the bank, and it will tie up④ our funds.

---

① payment terms 支付方式

② usual practice 惯例

③ deposit 存款；保证金

④ tie up 阻碍

K：Mr. Ellison，we may allow easier payment terms in the future，but for the first transaction，we have to insist on it.

E：If so，it seems that I have no choice. And when can you effect shipment?

K：Two months later，OK?

E：But，we are in urgent need of the goods for the New Year rush. Please do ship the goods next month.

K：Then，I will rearrange the production schedule for you. Shipment before September 20，can it be all right?

E：I think yes. I will report this to our director right now.

K：Thank you，Mr. Ellison. Wait for your good news. Goodbye!

E：Goodbye!

▶ Useful sentences

1. According to our usual practice，we require payment by confirmed，irrevocable L/C available by draft at sight.

根据我们的惯例，我们要求保兑的、不可撤销的、凭即期汇票支付的信用证。

2. We may allow easier payment terms in the future，but for the first transaction，we have to insist on it.

今后我们会允许更便利的支付方式，但是对于初次交易，我们只能坚持这种。

3. But，we are in urgent need of the goods for the New Year rush. Please do ship the goods next month.

但是，我们急需这些货物以赶上新年。请于下个月装运这些货物。

▶ Other useful sentences

1. Establishing business relations 建立业务关系

The purpose of my coming here is to talk business in toys.

我今天到此的目的是与你们进行玩具方面的洽商。

We deal in children's clothes and have been in this line for 8 years.

我们是经营童装的，干这行有 8 年了。

2. Enquiries and offers 询盘与报盘

May I know what particular items you are interested in?

我想知道你们对哪个产品感兴趣?

We can offer you 2,000 sets of electric fans at USD 5 per set CIFC2 New York.

我们可向你方提供 2 000 台电风扇的报价，每台 5 美元 CIF 纽约含 2% 的佣金。

3. Packing 包装

The packaging must be seaworthy and strong enough to stand rough handling.

包装必须适合海运，足够牢固，经得起粗鲁搬运。

4．Payment 支付

Could you possibly make an exception and accept a T/T transfer?

你们能否破例接受电汇付款?

We accept D/P only if the amount is under USD 2,000.

只有在数额不超过 2 000 美元的时候我们才接受付款交单。

5．Shipment 装运

I'm really sorry that we won't be able to make delivery within such a short time. It takes time to manufacture and pack the goods.

实在很抱歉，我们不能在这么短时间内发货。我们需要时间生产及包装货物。

I'm afraid I can't promise you July shipment because the shipping space for sailings to London has been booked up.

恐怕我们不能保证在 7 月份装运，因为到伦敦的舱位已经订完了。

6．Insurance 保险

We usually insure the goods against All Risks and War Risk for 110% of the invoice value.

我们通常按发票金额 110% 投保一切险和战争险。

Dialogue 3　Talking about the Agency

（K = Kary；E = Mr. Ellison，the customer in the first two dialogues. Since Mr. Ellison is quite satisfied with Kary's products，now he is talking with Kary about the idea of agency.）

E：First of all, I would be glad to tell you that my clients are quite satisfied with the several orders of your handbags. The styles and colors are very much to the taste[1] of our market.

K：I'm very glad to hear that, Mr. Ellison. So，there are more opportunities for us to cooperate，right?

E：That's the purpose of my coming to your company this time. I'd like to sign a sole agency agreement[2] with you on this item for a period of 3 years.

K：Mr. Ellison，we appreciate your good intention and effort in pushing the sale of our handbags. Then，could you give me your idea of the minimum annual[3] sales you can guarantee?

---

① to one's taste 合……口味

② sole agency agreement 独家代理协议

③ annual 每年的，一年的

E：I think we can ensure a turnover[1] of $10,000 annually within the area of the whole Australian market. And we expect a 5% commission.

K：It isn't a big amount, is it? We sold almost $15,000 last year in your market.

E：Well, I have to admit that we know very little about the areas outside the state of Victoria, which adds to the difficulty and expenses in our sales. It is a good policy to stand on the sage side, don't your agree?

K：Well, I agree. Let's put it this way. $12,000 to be sold in the first year, $15,000 in the second year, $17,000 in the third year, and the area is to be within Australia, commission 5%. OK?

E：That sounds fine. You will find us a most qualified agent.

K：I have no doubt about that. Let's talk about the details and arrange to sign an agency agreement.

E：Good.

▶ Useful sentences

1. I'd like to sign a sole agency agreement with you on this item for a period of 3 years.
我想与你们签订一份关于这项商品的 3 年的独家代理协议。

2. We appreciate your good intention and effort in pushing the sale of our handbags.
我们很感谢你们销售我方手袋的意愿以及在这方面所做的努力。

3. I think we can ensure a turnover of $ 10,000 annually within the area of the whole Australian market. And we expect a 5% commission.

我想我们能在整个澳大利亚市场内保证每年销售 1 万美元。同时我们要收取 5% 的佣金。

4. It is a good policy to stand on the sage side, don't your agree?
谨慎一点总是好事，你同意吗？

Listening Practice

You will hear 10 short sentences. Fill in the corresponding blanks according to what you've heard.

(1) The price of Pure Cotton Bed Sheet is US$ _____ per dozen.

(2) They will lower their price by _____ percent.

(3) Soda has a history of more than _____ years.

(4) The applicant for Sales Administrator is Mr. _____.

---

[1] turnover 营业额；成交量

（5）The net weight of the goods is _____ kilograms.

（6）The first branch of the BC Company started in _____.

（7）If you pay in Renminbi, the price is RMB _____ *yuan.*

（8）The last day for Mr. Lee to stay is _____ December.

（9）The sender of the parcel is Fred _____.

（10）_____ percent of the balance will be paid in local currency.

Culture Note

How Do You Communicate With Customers?

Here are a few ways to talk to your customers:

1. E-mail. E-mail can be used in several ways to connect with customers. For instance, you can send out a monthly newsletter for opted-in customers to keep up with company's updates or sales. Or better yet, send out a periodic survey to gather feedback from customers on their experiences working with you.

2. In Person. If you have a storefront, it's important not to discredit the brief conversation at the register. Even if the interaction is short, it's these conversations that will help customers remember the small business owner who chatted with them about their day.

3. Social Media. Social media is a great, easy way to communicate with customers. Whether it is engaging them through questions, or responding to customer service inquiries. It's also a great way for customers to share good experiences with other fans and get the word spread.

4. Direct Mail. Depending on the business you own, direct mail can be a useful way to get your message in front of your customer's face. Send them coupons for a special discount to get them back in your store, or on your website. For a special touch, you can send a personalized holiday card and thank them for working with you that year, for example.

Here are some notes we'd better pay attention to when we talk to our customers:

1. Demonstrate understanding. Take into account your customer's thoughts and concerns. When you speak to a customer, be aware of her personality and needs as a customer.

2. Repeat the message often. The message to your customer will be successful when you emphasize its most important aspects. Stress important features of your services and products.

3. Be aware of disruptions. The most successful communication happens when you

have the customer's complete attention. If you're in a public place (like your place of business), be sure to talk one on one and being away from other conversations. Loud music in your business can drown out ordinary conversations, so avoid it.

4. Provide practical details. Give customers information that helps them understand your products and services more fully.

5. Listen well. Accurately listening to your patrons is as important as talking to them. Efficient listening is giving careful attention to oral and nonverbal messages. Focus on what your customer is saying and his/her body language.

Pair Work

1. **Mr. Thomason and Mr. Zhang are talking about the price for Lady's dress. Mr. Thomason is the Purchasing Manager of Sunshine Trading Company, and Mr. Zhang is the Sales Representative of Pangshun Imp. & Exp. Company. Make a business conversation according to the information given.**

(T = Mr. Thomason, Z = Mr. Zhang)

T: Intend to place an order for Lady's dress, Item No. 5065, and ask for the lowest price, CIF Boston.

Z: Quote the price at US$ 25 per piece.

T: Bargain for a lower price and state the reasons.

Z: Support your price and state the reasons. And inquire about the quantity.

T: Express the intention for an order about 1,000 pieces.

Z: Offer a lower price for a bigger order.

2. **Your customer, Mr. Carpenter from Victory Appliance Store has placed an order for 600 air conditioners, Item No. KY – 02 with you (Kary), but this item is out of stock at the moment. So you recommend Item No. KY – 03. There are some instructions for both of you:**

Mr. Carpenter:

(1) Inquire about the available date for Item No. KY – 02.

(2) Ask for the details of Item No. KY – 03.

(3) Express the worries for the new item.

(4) Place a trial order for 300 sets.

You:

(1) Express regret for the unavailability of Item No. KY – 02.

(2) Recommend the similar and the latest Item No. KY – 03.

(3) Introduce the details and advantages of Item No. KY – 03.

(4) Introduce the sale conditions of Item No. KY – 03 in other markets.

Socializing Practice

▶ Situational Practice 1

Now you (Kary) have received Mr. White, your customer, at the airport, and you are accompanying him to the hotel. Make a short dialogue including the following points:

(1) About the weather for this time of the year in your city.

(2) The distance between the airport and the hotel.

(3) About your city's development, such as industry, economy, foreign trade, population and scenic places.

▶ Situational Practice 2

Compose a conversation according to the following information in pairs.

Mr. Frank's company has received your shipment of camera on time, but they complain that the goods are not the model they ordered. After you (Kary) check with the factory, you find that it's the mistake of the supplier, so you apologize. Mr. Frank needs an immediate delivery of the correct model and you agree. For the wrong consignment, you suggest Mr. Frank find another buyer for you, and you'll provide a 15% discount. Mr. Frank agrees.

▶ Situational Practice 3

洽谈内容：保险条款

地点：模拟公司谈判室

形式：口头洽谈

情景：

Mr. Charles from Brilliant Trading Company is asking something about the insurance of his order. Mr. Deng provides information in details as follows：

Commodity	Tea Sets
Insurance company	PICC
Insurance coverage	All Risks
Insured amount	110% of the invoice value
Claims payable at	Local city within 60 days after the arrival of the goods

要求：学生两人一组，根据给出的情景洽谈关于保险的事宜。洽谈要点如下（供参考）：

Mr. Charles	Mr. Deng
1. 询问保险公司	1. 告知保险公司
2. 询问投保险别	2. 告知投保险别，并解释承保范围
3. 要求增加战争险和罢工险	3. 同意但要对方支付额外保费
4. 询问投保金额及索赔地点、时间	4. 告知投保金额及索赔地点、时间

Daily Practice

▶▶ Tongue twister

1. Give me the gift of a grip top sock：a drip-drape，ship-shape，tip-top sock.

送我一对有紧袜带的袜子：悬挂状的、船形的、品质一流的袜子。

2. I slit a sheet，a sheet I slit. Upon the slitted sheet，I sit.

我撕开了一张纸，那张纸被我撕开了。在撕开了的纸上，我坐下了。

3. Say this sharply，say this sweetly，say this shortly，say this softly. Say this sixteen times in succession.

用斥责的语气说出这句话，用甜蜜的声音说出这句话，用最短的时间说出这句话，用温柔的声音说出这句话。将上述那段说话连续说 16 次。

4. Ruby Rugby's brother bought and brought her back some rubber baby-buggy bumpers.

鲁比勒比的哥哥买了一些四轮婴儿手推车的胶保险杠回来给她。

5. Fuzzy wuzzy was a bear. Fuzzy wuzzy had no hair. Fuzzy wuzzy wasn't fuzzy. Was he？

毛茸茸、软绵绵的是玩具熊。毛茸茸、软绵绵，一根头发也没有。毛茸茸、软绵绵的玩具熊并不毛茸茸，是吗？

▶▶ Read aloud

Ambition

It is not difficult to imagine a world short of ambition. It would probably be a kinder world：without demands，without abrasions，without disappointments. People would have time for reflection. Such work as they did would not be for themselves but for the collectivity. Competition would never enter in，conflict would be eliminated，tension would become a thing of the past. The stress of creation would be at an end. Art would no longer be troubling，but purely celebratory in its functions. Longevity would be increased，for fewer people would die of heart attack or stroke caused by tumultuous endeavor. Anxiety would be extinct. Time would stretch on and on, with ambition long departed from the human heart. Ah, how unrelieved boring life would be!

There is a strong view that holds that success is a myth, and ambition therefore a sham. Does this mean that success does not really exist? That achievement is at bottom empty? That the efforts of men and women are of no significance alongside the force of movements and events now. Not all success, obviously, is worth esteeming, nor all ambition is worth cultivating. Which are and which are not is something one soon enough learns on one's own. But even the most cynical secretly admit that success exists; that achievement counts for a great deal; and that the true myth is that the actions of men and women are useless. To believe otherwise is to take on a point of view that is likely to be deranging. It is, in its implications, to remove all motives for competence, interest in attainment, and regard for posterity.

We do not choose to be born. We do not choose our parents. We do not choose our historical epoch, the country of our birth, or the immediate circumstances of our upbringing. We do not, most of us, choose to die; nor do we choose the time or conditions of our death. But within all this realm of choicelessness, we do choose how we shall live: courageously or in cowardice, honorably or dishonorably, with purpose or in drift. We decide what is important and what is trivial in life. We decide that what makes us significant is either what we do or what we refuse to do. But no matter how indifferent the universe may be to our choices and decisions, these choices and decisions are ours to make. We decide. We choose. And as we decide and choose, so are our lives formed. In the end, forming our own destiny is what ambition is about.

Unit 6
Making Reservation and Appointments

Learning Objectives

Kary's boss is going to Shanghai to attend a meeting and meet an important client. Kary will reserve plane tickets and hotel for him. She also will make an appointment with the client. Her objectives are to master the basic words, expressions and useful sentences of making reservations and appointments; to learn the skills of making reservations and appointments. Kary's experiences will guide you through the essential elements of making reservations and appointments, which are widely used in society.

Warming-up

1. If you want to reserve[①] a plane ticket, what points will you pay attention to? List all the things you think are important while reserving. (time, class, price...)

2. If you want to reserve a hotel, what points will you pay attention to? List all the things you think are important while reserving. (time, transportation, price, service...)

3. If you want to make an appointment with someone, what points will you pay attention to? List all the things you think are important while reserving. (time, place, content...)

Kary's Story

Dialogue 1　Making Flight Reservation

(K = Kary, a Chinese businessperson; A = Airline Ticket Agent)

A: Good morning. What can I do for you?

K: Yes, I'd like to make a reservation to Shanghai next week.

---

① reserve 预定

A：When do you want to fly?

K：Tuesday, December 15th.

A：We have 9 flights① that day, 3 in the morning, 4 in the afternoon and 2 in the evening. What time do you prefer?

K：In the morning, around 10 o'clock.

A：OK. We have Flight MU5302. It departs② at 9：30 a. m. and arrives in Shanghai at 11：45 p. m. Is it OK?

K：Quite Good. That's it.

A：OK. Will this be round trip③ or one way?

K：Round trip returning on Friday.

A：So what time would you like to return that day?

K：Around 3 o'clock, please.

A：Let me check. (after several seconds) CZ3538, departs at 14：45 p. m. , arrives at 17：05 p. m. Is it OK?

K：OK.

A：Which would you prefer, first class④ or economy⑤?

K：First class, please. What's the fare⑥?

A：Totally, it is 3,880 *yuan*.

K：OK. I'll transfer⑦ money to you later.

A：Now could I have your name, please?

K：It's for my boss. His name is Robbie Williams. R-o-b-b-i-e, Robbie. W-i-l-l-i-a-m-s, Williams.

A：OK, I got it. Robbie Williams, will catch flight MU5302 at 9：30 a. m. on December 15th to Shanghai. And he will catch flight CZ3538 at 14：45 p. m. on December 18th back to Guangzhou. Both are first class.

K：Correct. Thanks!

A：My pleasure.

---

① flight 航班
② depart 离开，出发
③ round trip 双程
④ first class 头等舱
⑤ economy 经济舱
⑥ fare 费用，票价
⑦ transfer 转移

▶ Useful sentences

1. I'd like to make a reservation to Shanghai next week.

我想订一张下个星期去上海的机票。

I'd like to make a reservation to....

I want to book a seat to....

I'd like to reserve a seat to ...

2. When do you want to fly/depart?

你想什么时候出发?

3. Will this be round trip or one way?

单程还是双程呢?

4. Which would you prefer, first class or economy?

你是要头等舱还是经济舱呢?

▶ Other useful sentences

Customer：

1. I want a single ticket to Beijing tomorrow.

我想要一张明天去北京的单程票。

2. I'd like to leave between January 10th and 12th, do you have seats available?

我想 1 月 10 日到 12 日之间出发, 有位吗?

3. What flights do you have going to Beijing next Monday?

下周一到北京的航班有哪几个?

4. When will the flight take off/arrive?

航班是什么时候起飞/到达呢?

5. How long will it take?

这趟航班要飞多久呢?

6. I'd like to confirm① my plane reservation.

我想确定我预订的机票。

7. When is the next flight to Los Angeles? Is it full?

下一个去洛杉矶的航班是什么时候? 是满舱吗?

8. Are there seats available on the next flight?

下一个航班还有座位吗?

Agent clerk：

1. Which airline would you like to fly with?

您想乘坐哪家航空公司的航班呢?

_____

① confirm 确认, 证实

2. Could you wait a minute while I check availability?

您能稍等让我查一下是否有位吗？

3. Would you please check in one hour before departure?

请您在出发前一个小时登记好吗？

Dialogue 2　Making Hotel Reservation

（K = Kary；R = Receptionist of Sunshine Hotel）

R：Sunshine Hotel. Can I help you?

K：Yes, I'd like to book a single room for three nights, from December 15th to December 18th.

R：Just one moment. I'll check our room availability①. Yes, we have a single room available for those dates.

K：Is that on a smoking or non-smoking② floor?

R：We have both available. Which one do you prefer?

K：Smoking, please.

R：OK, not a problem. Could I have your name, please?

K：It's for my boss, Robbie Williams. R-o-b-b-i-e, Robbie. W-i-l-l-i-a-m-s, Williams.

R：Okay. What time will he arrive?

K：So will you offer③ airport pick-up service④?

R：Yes, we do offer. Could you tell me the arrival⑤ time and flight number?

K：The flight number is MU5302 and he will arrive at 11：45 p. m.

R：I see. We will pick up Mr. Williams at the airport on December 15th. He will stay for three nights in a single room on smoking floor.

K：That's true.

R：Can you give me your email address, please?

K：It's Kary0423@ yahoo. com.

R：Great. I'll email you a confirmation⑥ immediately. We look forward to Mr. Williams' arrival.

---

① availability 可得到的东西（人）

② non-smoking 无烟

③ offer 提供

④ pick-up service 接机服务

⑤ arrival 到达；抵达

⑥ confirmation 确认

▶ Useful sentences

1. I'd like to book a single room.

我想订一个单间。

2. Is that on a smoking or non-smoking floor?

是在无烟楼层还是吸烟楼层?

3. Will you offer airport pick-up service?

你们提供接机服务吗?

4. Can you give me your email address, please?

请给我你的邮箱地址好吗?

5. We look forward to Mr. Williams' arrival.

我们期待威廉姆斯先生的到来。

▶ Other useful sentences

1. I'd like to make a reservation for the third weekend in September.

我想预订9月第三个周末的房间。

2. Do you have any vacancies?

有空房吗?

3. What kind of room would you like to reserve?

请问您需要预定哪种类型的房间?

4. How about your hotel's facilities?

请问你们酒店有什么设施?

5. Which date would you like to book?

请问您想订哪一天?

6. What is the exact date of your arrival?

请问您确切的抵达日期是哪一天?

7. When will you check in and check out?

请问您什么时候入住和退房呢?

8. How long will you stay in our hotel?

请问您打算在我们酒店住多久呢?

9. How long will you be staying?

请问您打算住多久呢?

10. What is the rate, please?

请问房费是多少呢?

11. How many people is the reservation for?

会有多少人入住呢?

12. Would you like a room with twin beds or a double bed?

您的房间是需要两张单人床还是一张双人床呢?

13. Would you prefer to have a room with a view of the ocean?

您需要一间海景房吗?

14. Is there a phone number where you can be contacted?

请问有联系电话吗?

Dialogue 3　Making an Appointment

Kary is making an appointment with Alex Brown, the Marketing Manager of Shanghai Johnson Wax[①] *for her boss, Robbie Williams.*

(K = Kary; L = Linda, secretary of Alex Brown)

L: Hello, Linda speaking. What can I do for you?

K: Hello, Linda. This is Kary of Guangdong ABC Imp. & Exp. Corporation. I want to make an appointment with Mr. Brown for my boss, Mr. Williams. He will go to Shanghai to attend a meeting next week. It's a good chance to meet Mr. Brown in person on the contract[②] we will sign next month.

L: So when will Mr. Williams stay in Shanghai?

K: He will be free on the morning of Friday, December 18th. I am wondering if Mr. Brown is available[③] at that time.

L: Let me check the schedule. Please wait for me for several seconds. (after several seconds) Sorry for keeping you waiting. He will be free from 10 o'clock. Is it suitable?

K: Yes, good to him. So Mr. Williams will go to your company at 10 o'clock to meet Mr. Brown on Friday, December 18th.

L: Yes, we will be expecting him.

K: Wonderful. Thanks very much.

L: You are welcome. Goodbye.

K: Goodbye.

▶ Useful sentences

1. I want to make an appointment with Mr. Brown for my boss, Mr. Williams.

我想替我的老板威廉姆斯先生跟布朗先生预约。

2. It's a good chance to meet Mr. Brown in person on the contract we will sign next month.

———————————————

① Shanghai Johnson Wax 上海庄臣有限公司

② contract 合同

③ be available 有空

这是一个亲自与布朗先生会面商讨我们下个月即将签署的合同的好机会。

3.　I am wondering if Mr. Brown is available that time.

我想知道布朗先生那个时间有空吗？

4.　Sorry for keeping you waiting.

很抱歉让你久等了。

5.　We will be expecting him.

我们恭候他的光临。

▶ Other useful sentences

1.　I'm just phoning to see if we could fix① a meeting for next week.

我打电话是想看看我们能不能在下周约个时间见面。

2.　Could it be possible to see Mr. Brown sometime this week?

这个星期能不能和布朗先生见面？

3.　What time is convenient for him?

他什么时候有空呢？

4.　Could you make it a little later?

我们稍微晚一点，好吗？

5.　Anytime is fine.

随时都可以。

6.　I'll inform② you if there are any changes to our appointed time.

如果我们约定的时间有任何变化，我会告知你的。

7.　We look forward to meeting you then.

我们期待着那时候与您见面。

8.　Do you think I could meet the manager this afternoon?

今天下午我可以见到经理吗？

9.　Would it be convenient to see you on Friday morning?

周五上午见面方便吗？

10.　Will you be able to meet me some time tomorrow?

你能在明天某个时间和我会面吗？

11.　You'd better call the office to put off the appointment if there is something urgent.

如果有什么紧急事情的话，请打电话来推迟见面。

---

① fix 安排，决定（某事）
② inform 通知，告知

Tips：

Skills of Making Business Calls

1. Make calls during the normal business hours.

2. The most significant thing is making business calls correctly and smartly. So the professional preparation is necessary. First, prepare the stationery, such as: memo for taking down details, different colour pencils to mark different matters, suitable locations of items on the desk (put telephone on the left, memo on the right).

3. Before making calls, be clear about your purpose and sort out① the thought.

4. While making calls, speak in a professional manner. For example, state your name directly when picking up calls to save time and improve the efficiency.

5. While making calls, be polite. Treat the callers as you would like to be treated; treat the callers as they would like to be treated.

6. While making calls, be brief and to the point②.

7. While making calls, make sure your sound upbeat③ and optimistic④.

Listening Practice

You are going to hear 3 conversations. As you listen, decide which answer is correct.

▶ Conversation 1

1. What flight does the man take actually?

A. The 8:30 flight.

B. The 10:30 flight.

C. The 9:30 flight.

2. What do you know about the flight at 8:30?

A. The tickets were all sold out.

B. It has changed its taking-off time.

C. The plane is too crowded.

▶ Conversation 2

1. What time will Sara go to the restaurant?

---

① sort out 解决（问题）；理清（细节）

② to the point 中肯，扼要

③ upbeat 愉快的，高兴的

④ optimistic 乐观的

A. 7 o'clock.

B. 2 o'clock.

C. 7: 20.

2. What's Sara's special requirement?

A. Smoking seats.

B. A table by the window.

C. A table near the door.

▶ Conversation 3

1. Does the caller reserve rooms?

A. Yes.

B. No.

C. Not sure.

2. How many rooms does the caller reserve?

A. The caller reserved one room.

B. The caller reserved two rooms.

C. The caller reserved three rooms.

3. What's the name of the hotel?

A. Hotel Carinthia.

B. Hotel Tauernblick.

C. Grand Park Hotel.

4. For how long does the guest stay there?

A. Three nights.

B. Four nights.

C. Five nights.

Culture Note

Types of Reservations

In United States culture, there are several different types of reservations. The word can be used to describe something that is set aside for a person or a group of people or it can used to describe uncertainty or doubt. Typical reservations that are meant to be set aside for people are booking reservations, land reservations and legal rights reservations. Uncertainty or doubt can be defined as a mental reservation.

1. Booking Reservations

A booking reservation can apply to restaurants, hotels, transportation, such as airplanes, cruises and trains and seating at an event. The fundamental idea of this type of reservation is that seating or rooms are held for you and your party. To make a booking reservation you must call ahead and tell the business what seats you would like or what type of room you would like. The business will reserve this for you so it will be available upon arrival.

2. Mental Reservations

Mental reservations refer to doubt at the back of a person's mind. A person with mental reservations may be unable to make a concrete decision in a situation with multiple possibilities. For example, if a person has the chance to invest in a project that could make a large return or could just leave him nothing, he may have mental reservations, or doubt about making the investment. Because of his reservations, he may be unable to make the decision of whether or not to invest.

3. Land Reservations

Land reservations refer to land set aside for a particular use. A nature reservation may preserve natural wildlife by prohibiting construction. Nature reservations are often managed by states, federal government agencies and private groups. In the United States, American Indian reservations are sections of land set aside for Native American communities. Native Americans are able to live within a separate society with separate laws, within reason. For example, casinos can be legal on Indian reservations. Because casinos are prohibited or regulated in most places in the United States, American Indian reservations attract much tourism from casinos.

4. Legal Reservation of Rights

In American law, the reservation of rights is a statement of a person or business retaining and using its legal rights. Reservation of rights statements are often used as a copyright notice or by insurance companies. The reservation of rights for copyright law is the statement "all rights reserved" printed next to the date of the copyrighted material. This statement is meant to warn people of the penalties of copying or stealing the copyrighted material. The reservation of rights for insurance companies is a letter to an insured person stating that the company may deny a claim. If the insurance company denies the claim, they will cite the sent reservation of rights letter.

(By Marianne Luke)

Pair Work

Pair Work 1

Student A:

You are making a call to book a flight to Beijing as soon as possible. It's

9: 10 a. m. now.

Student B:

You are the staff of airline ticket agent. There are five flights to Beijing in the morning that day.

Flight	Departure	Fare	Status
CZ3101	10: 30	¥ 1, 040	Full
CA1310	10: 45	¥ 1, 190	Over 10 tickets left
HU7804	11: 20	¥ 990	2 tickets left
CZ3099	11: 45	¥ 950	3 tickets left
CZ3120	12: 00	¥ 969	5 tickets left

▶ Pair Work 2

Student A:

You are calling to Linda to make an appointment on Tuesday afternoon. You are also free on Wednesday afternoon.

Student B:

You are Linda. You will have an important meeting on Tuesday afternoon. But you are free on Wednesday afternoon.

Socializing Practice

▶ Role-play

Choose the hotel

Student A:

Imagine that your company is going to send you a business trip to Hangzhou. The place you will work is near Wulin Square. As the limitation of money (300 RMB/day), you have to call three hotels to decide which one to live. Besides the money, you should consider the location, transportation and other elements.

Student B:

You are the receptionist of Sunshine Hotel. You will answer the call according to the following information:

● Introduction

Sunshine Hotel, a stylish hotel designed by a famous designer, is located in the commercial center of Gongshu District. Across from JUSCO, it is only a few steps to Beijing-Hangzhou Grand Canal. Sunshine hotel's services are offered to meet the needs of each guest and are full of pleasant surprise. Throughout the hotel, the complimentary wired and wireless high-speed broadband Internet access enables guests to stay connected with friends, family and work.

- Room type & price

Room type	Breakfast	Price
Delicate City View Room	No	¥348
Deluxe City View Twin Room	No	¥398
Delicate Lake View Room	Yes	¥448

Student C:

You are the receptionist of Hangzhou Hotel. You will answer the call according to the following information:

- Introduction

Located at the CBD of Hangzhou—the southern part of Wulin Square, Hangzhou Hotel is a high star hotel which integrates accommodations, food & beverages, entertainment and business services.

Hangzhou Hotel is only 1km from the famous West Lake. As one of the landmark Hangzhou Hotel is 112 meters. There are 32 floors and some of them are non-smoking floors that build an eco-friendly environment. Broadband Internet access is available in all 223 guest rooms. Central air-conditionings and digital televisions are equipped in all rooms.

- Room type & price

Room type	Breakfast	Price
Standard Twin Room	Yes	¥398
Single Room	Yes	¥428
Business Twin Room	Yes	¥458

Student D:

You are the receptionist of Castle Hotel. You will answer the call according to the following information:

- Introduction

Castle hotel is located in Hangzhou, with the transportaion convenience of a 5-minute walk to Wulin Square. Subway Line No.3 is next door. The hotel has 150 units of luxurious rooms, including standard rooms, triple rooms, and business suites. Every suit has 32 ~ 40 LCD TV, complimentary wired and wireless Internet access.

- Room type & price

Room type	Breakfast	Price
Superior Single Room	No	￥288
Special Standard Room	No	￥318
Deluxe King Room	No	￥358

Task 1：

1. Based on the standard offered by the company, Student A makes three calls to different hotels to get the information about the hotel in details. With regard to the transportation, price and the service, student A can list the questions first, then make the phone calls.

2. The other 3 students will read the information carefully. They will answer the questions in details according to the card. If there is no obvious information to answer questions, they can answer according to their experience or imagination.

3. After finishing the 3 calls, student A decides which one to live.

4. Students A makes phone call to the hotel which he/she chose to make a reservation.

Task 2：

1. Discuss in groups.

2. Student A tells others the reason why he/she choose _____ hotel.

3. The group members finish a presentation on "Why I choose _____ hotel" together.

4. The reporter gives the presentation one group by another.

5. Evaluate each other's performance.

Daily Practice

▶ Tongue twister

1. Few free fruit flies fly from flames.

没有几只果蝇从火焰中飞过去。

2. Fresh fried fish, fish fresh fried, fried fish fresh, fish fried fresh.

新鲜的油炸鱼，鲜鱼被油炸，油炸的鱼很新鲜，油炸的鲜鱼。

3. Of all the felt I ever felt, I never felt a piece of felt which felt as fine as that felt felt, when first I felt that felt hat's felt.

在我所触摸过的毡子中，我从未触摸过一块如此舒适的毡子，直至我试过这顶毡帽为止。

4. There is no need to light a night light on a light night like tonight, for a bright night

light is just like a slight light.

像今夜这样明亮的夜晚，不需要点一盏夜灯，因为明亮的夜灯也会变得微弱。

5. There was a young lady from Niger, who smiled as she rode on a tiger. They returned from the ride with the lady inside and the smile on the face of the tiger.

从前有个年轻的女士，她来自尼日尔。她骑在老虎上，露出微笑。他们骑虎结束后返了回来，这时那位女士已经到了老虎肚子里。老虎的脸上露出微笑。

▶ Read aloud

Seven Things Never to Say on a Business Call

It's the 21st century. Do you know how your employees answer the phone? Good phone manners have always been important, of course. Yet too few companies make any effort to train employees in phone etiquette, says Nancy Friedman, president and founder of the Telephone Doctor, a St. Louis-based customer service training company. The result is often losting business, irritating customers and squandering opportunities, she says.

So, if you want to keep and add customers, keep your employees from saying these things on the phone.

1. "That's not our policy." This popular excuse to avoid taking action on complaints or requests is not only poor manners. It's also damaging. Who cares what is or isn't "policy"? What dolt sets it? Think: How can any company policy rationalize hanging up on dissatisfied customers? If an employee cannot grant the request or fix the complaint, he or she ought to consult a superior for advice or be given authority to find alternatives that will transform the customer from dissatisfied to appreciative. Either way, keep the customer informed at every stage.

2. "That's not my department." or "That's not my job." Everyone and anyone working for the company must be prepared to meet any and every caller's needs. At the very least, if the employee lacks knowledge or responsibility, he or she should get a phone number, ask a manager for help and call back, expeditiously, with information that does the trick.

3. "Could you call back? We're really busy right now." This one boggles the business mind. But employees say it more often than you'd think. It always makes me wonder: Busy with what? Lunch dates? Make sure no staffer you hire ever gets away with saying anything even close to this.

4. "My computer's down," or "We're having trouble with our servers." This is simply not a caller's problem, nor a reason to suspend service. Business runs with or without active monitors. Even if the caller is a supplier that you hire and fire, apologize for the fact that you cannot help. Then pick up a pencil, write down the phone number, and (read this carefully) get back to him or her as soon as you can help — unfailingly.

5. "I was just waiting to get more information before calling you back." Everyone

knows this is a ploy. If you were really gathering info, you'd send an interim e-mail or leave an explanatory voice mail—which is what every experienced client does with important contacts. All this phrase does is to insult the caller by signaling that he or she has no priority in your schedule—or else that you're incompetent. Either way, if you're avoiding someone's calls, be more creative.

6. "I'll see that she calls you." This is pure self-protection. "You should only promise to deliver the message, not that there will be a return call," Friedman says. It's not up to you to promise someone else's attention. If there is no return call, you've created unnecessary disappointment or irritation.

7. "I just buried my mother." Honestly, I wouldn't have thought it necessary to tell anyone not to mention personal tragedies during business calls. Never bring your personal problems into business conversations, unless you have a long-term and personal friendship with the caller.

Every time an employee picks up a receiver, the possibility of gaining or losing business is on the line. Make sure your opportunities don't go unanswered.

(By Joanna L. Krotz)

Unit 7   Dealing with Daily Affairs

Learning Objectives

In the company, Kary are supposed to do some daily affairs. Her objectives are to master the basic words, expressions and useful sentences of making polite receptions, seeking for① help and raising requirements; to learn the skills of using some office equipment following the instructions②. Kary's experiences will guide you through the essential③ elements of raising requirements and asking for helps, which are widely used in society.

Warming-up

1. If you receive a guest, what points will you pay attention to? List all the things you think are important while receiving guest. (manner, language...)

2. What are the commonly used equipment in a modern office? (fax machine④, copier⑤, printer⑥, scanner⑦, paper shredder⑧...)

3. If you want to use the fax machine, what can you do if you don't know? (ask for help, read the instruction...)

---

① seek for 寻求
② instruction 说明书
③ essential 必要的
④ fax machine 传真机
⑤ copier 复印机
⑥ printer 打印机
⑦ scanner 扫描仪
⑧ paper shredder 碎纸机

Kary's Story

Dialogue 1   Receiving Guests

(K = Kary, a Chinese businessperson; W = Wang Jun, a guest)

K: Good morning. What can I do for you?

W: Good morning. I want to meet your manager, Mr. Williams.

K: Do you have an appointment?

W: Yes, I have.

K: May I have your name, please?

W: I'm Wang Jun from Five Stars Advertising Company.

K: Would you please have a seat and wait for seconds. I'll see if he is available.

W: All right.

(after several seconds)

K: I'm terribly sorry. Mr. Williams is busy at this moment. Would you please wait for a moment and have a cup of coffee? And he will be free in a few minutes.

W: OK, thank you for your coffee. By the way, can I meet Mr. White, the manager of Human Resource Department later?

K: Do you have an appointment with him?

W: No, I don't have.

K: So please wait a moment. I'll call to his secretary to see if he is free now.

W: OK, thanks a lot!

(after a while)

K: I felt so sorry. He is on business trip this week.

W: That's a pity! Never mind, I will make an appointment with his secretary next time.

K: OK. (receive a call) Mr. Wang, Mr. Williams is free now and he is expecting you. Please go this way!

W: That's good. Thank you again!

K: You're welcome.

▶ Useful sentences

1. Do you have an appointment?

请问您约好了吗?

2. May I have your name, please?

请问您贵姓？

3．Would you please have a seat and wait for seconds.

请您坐下稍等片刻。

4．I'll see if he is available.

我看看他是否方便。

5．Would you please wait for a moment and have a cup of coffee?

你能再等会儿吗？喝杯咖啡怎么样？

6．And he will be free in a few minutes.

他一会儿就有空了。

7．He is expecting you.

他正在等你。

▶ Other useful sentences

1．What company are you from?

您是哪个公司的？

2．Could you tell me what company you are representing①?

能告诉我您代表哪家公司吗？

3．Can I ask what you wish to see him about?

我能问一下您有什么事要见他吗？

4．Would you give me your business card?

请给我您的名片好吗？

5．Would you like coffee or tea? How do you like your coffee?

您要咖啡还是茶？要什么样的咖啡呢？

6．Please have a seat. Mr. Williams will come in a few minutes.

请坐，威廉姆斯先生几分钟就到。

7．Mr. Williams, Mr. Wang from ABC Company want to see you for a few moments. May I bring him in?

威廉姆斯先生，ABC 公司的王先生想见您，我可以让他进来吗？

8．Mr. Williams is busy at the moment and he will not be free today.

威廉姆斯先生现在很忙，而且他今天也没有时间。

9．Mr. Williams is occupied at the moment and wants to know if your business is urgent.

威廉姆斯先生现在很忙，请问您的事情很紧急吗？

———————————

① represent 代表

10. Would you please tell me your telephone number so I can ring you up to arrange[①] an appointment?

您可以把您的电话号码告诉我吗? 我安排好后打电话通知您。

11. If you would be kind enough to let me know in advance[②] the date and approximate[③] time of any intended visit, I will make arrangements to receive you.

如果能提前告知计划来访日期及大概时间，我会安排接待您的。

12. If I can do anything for you, please let me know.

如果我能为您做什么，尽管说好了。

Dialogue 2　Using the Fax Machine

Mr. Williams asks Kary to fax a document to Wang Jun after he met him. But Kary doesn't know how to use the fax machine.

(K = Kary; J = Jack, her colleague)

K: Jack, sorry to bother you. Can you show me how to use the fax machine?

J: It's my pleasure. Kary, come over here. Let me show you how to operate[④] it.

K: OK. It's so kind of you. This fax machine looks complicated[⑤].

J: First of all, don't worry about all these buttons[⑥].

K: Yes.

J: Actually, it's not difficult. The first thing you have to do is to make sure that there's thermal paper[⑦] in it.

K: Sure.

R: The next thing you do is to insert[⑧] the documents what you want to fax into this slot[⑨], right here, see?

K: Yes.

J: Put it face down. It's very important. Remember this point. And since the size of

---

① arrange 安排

② in advance 提前

③ approximate 大概

④ operate 操作

⑤ complicated 复杂的

⑥ button 按钮

⑦ thermal paper 热敏纸

⑧ insert 插入

⑨ slot 狭槽

paper is different，you can adjust^① this little thing.

K：I see.

J：Now，if you are ready，you can dial the number of the receiver of documents. And then，when you hear the receiving signal^②，press the "send" button. That's all. Is that clear?

K：Yes，I'm sure I can use it now. By the way，how can I know if my fax is sent?

J：You can set up the fax machine to print a completion^③ receipt^④. It will also print an error^⑤ page if the fax does not go through.

K：I see. And do we have a fax template^⑥ of the company?

J：We do. I will send you an electronic^⑦ copy later.

K：Thanks a lot.

J：You're welcome!

▶ Useful sentences

1. Sorry to bother you.

很抱歉打扰你了。

2. Can you show me how to use the fax machine?

你能教我怎么用传真机吗?

3. Let me show you how to operate it.

我给你展示一下怎么操作。

4. It's so kind of you.

你人真好。

5. This fax machine looks complicated.

这台传真机看起来很复杂。

6. The first thing you have to do is to make sure that there's thermal paper in it.

首先你要做的是确定机器里有热敏纸。

7. The next thing you do is to insert the documents what you want to fax into this slot。

接下来，你把你要传真的文件放在这个卡槽内。

8. Put it face down.

---

① adjust 调整

② signal 信号

③ completion 完成

④ receipt 回执；收据

⑤ error 错误

⑥ template 模板

⑦ electronic 电子的

正面朝下放。

9.　If you are ready, you can dial the number of the receiver of documents.　And then, when you hear the receiving signal, press the "send" button.

如果你准备好了，就拨通文件接收方的传真号。当你收到接收的信号时，按下发送按钮就可以了。

10.　By the way, how can I know if my fax is sent?

对了，我怎么知道传真是否发送出去了呢？

11.　You can set up the fax machine to print a completion receipt.

你可以设定传真机打印一张完成回执.

12.　It will also print an error page if the fax does not go through.

如果传真发送失败的话，传真机也会打印一张发送失败回执。

13.　And do we have a fax template of the company?

我们公司有统一的传真格式吗？

▶ Other useful sentences

1.　I need to send a fax.　Do you have a cover page with the company logo?

我要发个传真，你有带公司标志的封面吗？

2.　What's the importance of the date, time and serial numbers[1] printed on the top of the fax?

传真上方的日期、时间和序列号为什么那么重要啊？

3.　The memory of the fax machine is full, and there is no paper to print.

传真机的内存已经满了，而且也没有打印纸了。

4.　Place the papers face down on the paper tray[2].

将纸张正面朝下放到送纸匣上。

5.　If you have a paper jam[3], make sure you clear the jammed paper properly.

如果卡纸，你要确定适当地将卡纸清除。

6.　The documents fed into the fax machine were scanned and came out in the return tray.

文件放入传真机会被扫描然后送出到文件回收匣。

Dialogue 3　Talking about Using E-mail

Kary is making a call to Wang Jun to make sure if he receives the documents and decide

---

① serial number 序列号

② tray 托盘

③ paper jam 卡纸

the way of further① communication.

（K = Kary；W = Wang Jun）

K：Hello，this is Kary speaking. May I speak to Wang Jun?

W：Speak，please.

K：I faxed the documents to you just now. Have you read it?

W：Yes，I have.

K：Mr. Williams said he need to know more about that project. Would you please offer me some more information?

W：Sure. But how can I send it to you? By EMS?

K：No，it's not convenient. You can send it by e-mail.

W：So may I have your e-mail address?

K：Yes，please write it down. It's Kary0423@ yahoo. com.

W：Kary0423@ yahoo. com，right?

K：Right.

W：OK，I will send it immediately，and you can check it out in a few minutes.

K：Thank you very much！

W：You're welcome. Goodbye.

K：Goodbye.

▶ Useful sentences

1. Would you please offer me some more information?
您能提供我更多的信息吗？

2. May I have your e-mail address?
能告诉我你的邮箱地址吗？

3. I will send it immediately，and you can check it out in a few minutes.
我马上发邮件，你一会儿就可以去查收了。

▶ Other useful sentences

1. Can you show me how to make an attachment② with our e-mail program?
你能教教我怎样在邮件程序中粘贴附件吗？

2. I'll send it along to you as soon as I get back to the office.
我一回到办公室就给你发过去。

3. I will be sure to e-mail the information to your address as soon as possible tomorrow morning.

---

① further 进一步的

② attachment 附件

我明天早上尽快把信息发到你的信箱。

4. Since there are many opportunities to work together in the future, we'd better keep in touch① by e-mail.

既然将来有很多合作机会，我们最好用电子邮件保持联系。

5. I am especially interested in your project. Can you e-mail the details to me?

我对你的计划很感兴趣，能发细节给我吗？

6. I can't use my computer to send e-mails. I'll ask our technical support for some help.

我的电脑不能发邮件了，我要去找技术人员帮忙。

7. I want to set up an e-mail account.

我想申请个电子邮件账户。

8. My e-mail can't get through.

我的邮件发不出去。

9. Can you help me to check the e-mail?

能帮我查收一下邮件吗？

Tips:

As a salesperson, reception is one of the most important routine jobs. Here are some rules of reception etiquette② you can follow:

1. Smile when greeting the visitor, showing gladness to see each other.

2. Always stand up to greet and shake hands with visitors.

3. While shaking hands, be brief, firm and warm. Be accompanied by a direct look into the eyes of visitors.

4. Stop your telephone conversation immediately when there are some visitors.

5. Offer your visitors something to drink. (e. g. water, coffee, tea)

6. Remain calm and patient at all times even if callers or visitors express frustration or anger.

7. Avoid holding phone calls (except in an emergency③).

8. Don't make a visitor feel to be forgotten or ignored.

9. Apologize to the visitor when you have to keep him/her waiting.

10. When the visitor is to leave, you had better go with him/her as far as the door of the office or the elevator.

---

① keep in touch 保持联系

② etiquette 礼仪

③ emergency 紧急情况

Listening Practice

You are going to hear Kary speaking about being a receptionist，please fill in the blanks while listening.

Obviously we use a _____ , a _____ , and printers；I think we have about _____ different printers in this office that I use on a daily basis. I also use a _____ system. Sometimes those can be pretty complicated. You've got to really know _____ to use it. They often come with a manual. _____ we had our telephone system replaced here a _____ months ago，I actually had to spend about _____ hours going through the manual figuring out how to program it，figuring out how to program everyone else's _____ , intercom buttons，things like that. You've got to know how to _____ a phone call. Really，that's your main job being a front line phone person for transferring calls to voice mail or other _____ , jobs like that. Also you've got to know how to use a _____ . If you don't know how to use a computer，you're in _____ because I will tell you _____ % of receptionist and secretarial positions require PC knowledge. You've got to know how to use basic _____ such as those in Microsoft Office：Excel，_____ , Word and Outlook which is a big one for _____ .

Culture Note

About Business Etiquette

Business etiquette changes over time. For instance，there was a time when women were not allowed to wear pants to a business meeting. The strategy is to keep pace with the times and read literature regarding the topic. Today，there are not as many strict clothing guidelines，but there are still some social faux pas①. Overall，etiquette incorporates behavior and appearance. This translates to interoffice workplace matters，business presentations and introductions to new people，to name a few.

Behavior

Part of business etiquette includes exhibiting the correct behavior in various situations. According to the Grad View website，when you take a cab，you should make sure your client or boss will step out of the car on the curb side and won't have to get out in traffic or slide across the seat. This establishes that the client or boss is valued and important.

When dining out for business，your table manners become important. You should know

---

① faux pas 失礼；失言

how much to tip a waiter and when to season food. The behavior will indicate your social status, education and your competency to handle the job. Typically, the tip rate is 15 percent of the total bill, and you should season the food only after tasting it. Brush up on other table manners, such as the correct use of cutlery, wine glasses and napkins. Making a good impression with proper etiquette can go a long way, and set the business relationship off to a good start.

Appearance

Knowing what to wear and how to appear are vital to sealing the deal. Wear something conservative to avoid any distractions. Dark colors work best because they denote seriousness. Bold colors may be out of place, but you can always loosen up during a later meeting, if appropriate. Bring a light briefcase or portfolio bag to finish the polished look. Avoid chewing gum during any meeting. Confirm the meeting a day before, and arrive 15 to 30 minutes early. It may be that your client arrives early too, so be ready for small talk. Maintain a well groomed appearance that presents you as a professional. For more information about appearance, contact a local university career center for tips. They often offer assistance to alumni, and sometimes to the business community. They are great resources for mock interviews and other interpersonal skills that deal with outward appearance and behavior.

(By Jamie M. Kisner, eHow Contributor)

Pair Work

▶ Task 1

There is a dialogue between the secretary and uninvited guest.

Student A:

You are Kary, a sales person wants to see your boss, Mr. Williams. Your boss doesn't want to meet him. You are going to talk to Student B, try to explain that Mr. Williams cannot meet him/her.

Student B:

You are a sales person. You want to meet Mr. Williams without an advanced appointment. You are going to talk to Student A, try to convince him/her to let you meet Mr. Williams.

▶ Task 2

There is a dialogue happened in the office about fax. You will see the paragraphs in disorder. Each of you will have 4 paragraphs. First you should read the paragraphs carefully and then discuss the paragraphs in your hand then arrange the order of the paragraphs into a complete dialogue.

Student A:

Paragraph 1: I guess the fax machine is out of paper too. Don't worry, I'll have someone look at it this afternoon, and in the meantime, I'll have your document refaxed to our other fax machine.

Paragraph 2: What about that one?

Paragraph 3: Did you put this morning's faxes on my desk? I'm waiting for some urgent faxes from headquaters. I'm pretty sure they came in last night.

Paragraph 4: You know, I think the fax machine is out of toner. I can change the toner cartridge. That should solve the problem.

Student B:

Paragraph 5: Yes, but this one will have to be refaxed as well. And look, there's about 3 pages missing. It looks like the fax machine ate half of my important faxes, and ones that made it through are so blurred or too light. They are unreadable.

Paragraph 6: Yeah, you're going to have to call them and get them to be refaxed. These copies are so dark. I can't make out any of the words.

Paragraph 7: This one? This one is so light that I can barely read it. How can that be?

Paragraph 8: Everything that came in the office fax machine last night is all on your desk, but I noticed that some of the faxes came through pretty blurred. Maybe you take a look at them if the copy is unreadble. I'll call them and ask them to refax.

The order is: ____→____→____→____→____→____→____→____

Socializing Practice

▶ Role-play

You are Mr. /Miss "Know all"!

Student A:

You are the "know all" in your company. If your colleagues have any problems with the equipment, they will ask you for help. Here, you will help three colleagues.

● Instructions for the use of paper shredder

How to use:

1. To switch on, press the green button.

2. Put the paper in.

3. To switch off, press the red button.

Possible problems and the solutions:

Problem: The machine jams.

Solution: Press the red button. Remove the excess paper and start again.

Problem: The motor overheats.

Solution: The machine switches off automatically. Leave it for 15 ~ 30 minutes to cool down. And then switch on again.

Caution:

Do not put your fingers into the shredder.

Be careful with long hair and loose clothing.

● Instructions for the use of scanner

Use the SCAN DOCUMENT TO button ( ) to scan documents.

1. Place the originals face down on the scanner glass or face up in the ADF. If you are scanning two-sided originals from an ADF, slide the DUPLEX switch to two-sided mode ( ).

2. Select a destination by pressing the DESTINATION button ( ) until the desired destination appears in the front panel display.

3. Press the SCAN DOCUMENT TO button ( ).

(Note: A preview image will not appear when scanning from the ADF. To change this preview setting, see the Hp Photo & Imaging Software Help.)

4. Select the final scan area (the area inside the dotted lines) in the preview image.

5. Make adjustments to the preview image if needed.

6. Click Accept.

The final scan area is scanned and appears in the specified destination.

● Instructions for use of copier

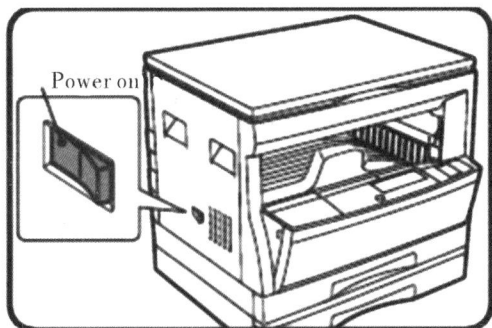

1. Turn the power switch on.

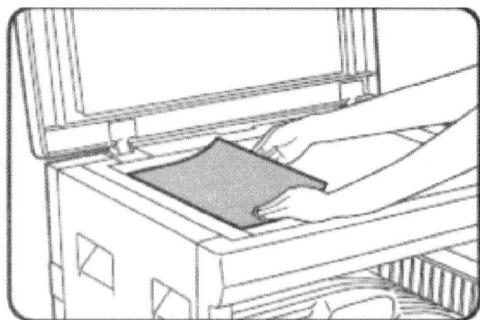

2. Place the original face down on the original table. Align it with the original size scale.

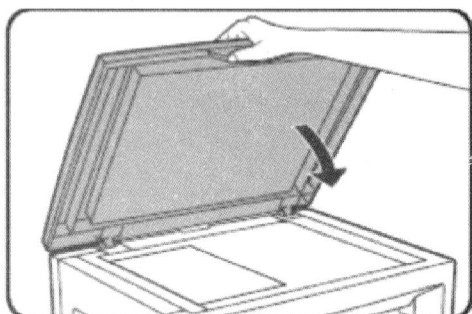

3. Close the platen cover.

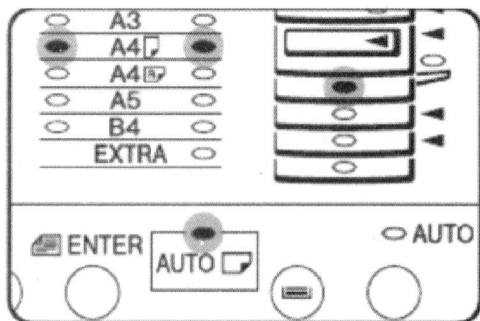

4. Ensure that the desired paper tray is selected.

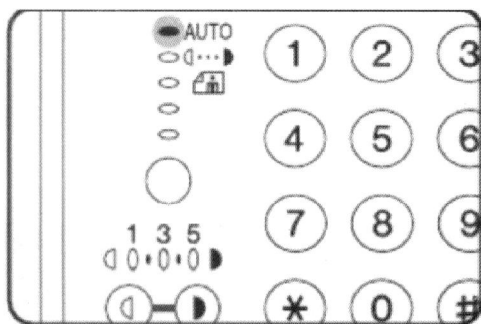

5. Adjust the copy density. Auto exposure is the standard initial seeing for this copier.

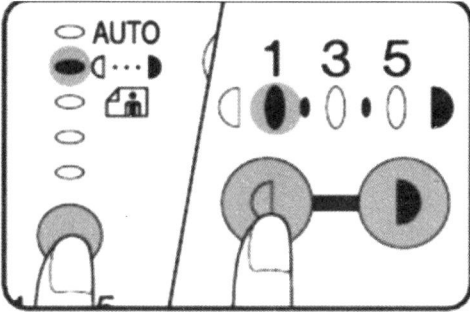

6. For manual copy density adjustment, press the AUTOMANUAL/PHOTO key to select and adjust with the light and dark keys as desired.

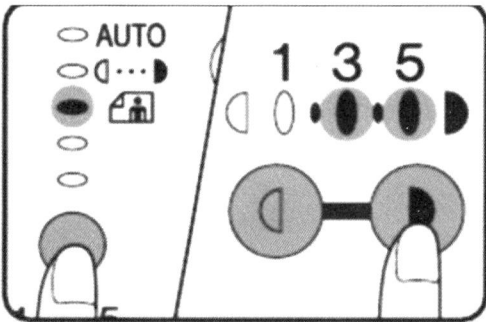

7. For photographs, select PHOTO and then adjust with the light and dark keys as desired.

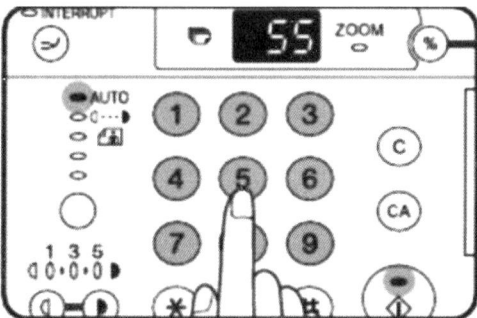

8. Set the number of copies using the numeric keys.

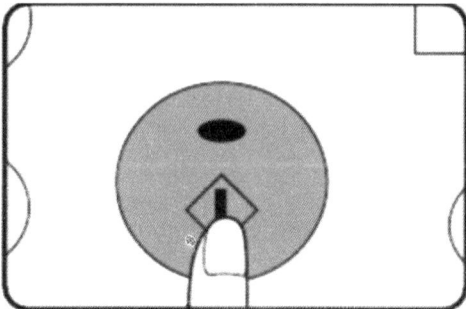

9. Press the start key.

Student B：

You are going to use the paper shredder, but you can't find the operation instructions for it. You ask student A for help.

Student C：

You are going to use the scanner, but you can't find the operation instructions for it. You ask student A for help.

Student D：

You are going to use the copier, but you can't find the operation instructions for it. You ask student A for help.

Task：

Step 1：

Student A tries to be familiar with the instructions of the three equipment.

Student B, C and D decide what questions they are going to ask student A.

Step 2：

Make conversations between these four people. The best Mr. / Miss "Know all" will be chosen by all the students.

Daily Practice

▶ Tongue twister

1. The soldiers shouldered shooters on their shoulders.

士兵们用肩膀顶着发射装置。

2. If you notice this notice you will notice that this notice is not worth noticing.

若你看到这张告示，你会发现这张告示是不值得留意的。

3. While we were walking, we were watching window washers wash Washington's windows with warm washing water.

当我们走路时，我们看着清洁窗户的人用暖水清洗华盛顿的窗户。

4. Swan swam over the sea, swim, swan swim! Swan swam back again well swum, swan!

天鹅游到海的另一边。游吧！天鹅游吧！天鹅游回来了！游得真好啊！天鹅！

5. Pick a partner and practise passing, for if you pass proficiently, perhaps you'll play professionally.

选择一位队员练习传球，如果你能熟练地传球，你或许会成为一位专业球员。

6. I thought a thought. But the thought I thought wasn't the thought I thought I thought.

我思考一个问题。可是，我所思考的问题并不是我认为自己正在思考的问题。

Remember These "Don'ts" in the Office

Work is the place where we spend most of our time, but we don't really get to choose whom we spend that time with. Some coworkers are courteous and fun, while some are so obnoxious that we tell stories about them years later.

Most people at any place of business are just trying to do their work and get through the day with the minimum amount of drama. To ensure that the water-cooler conversation stays focused on last night's TV program and not on you, avoid these cringe-worthy behaviors.

1. Leave Your Personal Life at Home

As long as your office permits it, it's natural to take a few personal calls during the workday, or to occasionally use the shared printer to print out a recipe or an interesting article from the Internet. Just don't make your cubemates listen to extended phone conversations with your spouse, or litter the equipment area with printouts of your vacation pictures and faxes from your doctor's office. To your coworkers (and your boss), it can seem as if you spend more time on personal business than you do actually working.

2. Don't Make Yourself at Home

Every office has its own level of formality and its own set of unspoken rules of decorum, but some things are non-negotiable. It may be okay to toss off your stilettos while you're working at your desk, but don't walk around the office barefoot. The dress code might be casual, but that doesn't usually expand to include pajama pants or Crocs.

3. Mind Your Cell Phone Manners

If you need to take or make an extended call on your cell phone, either step outside or go to a quiet area so that your coworkers aren't distracted by the conversation. Also make sure to keep your phone's ringer set quiet or vibrant. Nothing's more annoying than having to listen to someone's phone playing a "Love Shack" ringtone over and over because she's in a meeting and can't answer it.

4. Stay Home If You're Ill

Everyone appreciates dedication, but if you can't make it through the day without coughing, wheezing, sneezing, or retching, just stay home. Not only can it be distracting to spend all day listening to the sounds of illness, but no matter how much Lysol you spray around your desk, you're bound to leave some germs around, and your coworkers don't want to get sick. When you feel genuinely rotten, do everyone a favor and take a sick day.

5. Be Brief in the Bathroom

While few people would object to their coworkers' flossing after meals or touching up makeup before leaving for the day, the bathroom is not a place to hang out in interminably. It's not a place in which to have private conversations with another coworker, engage in plucking, tweezing, or other kinds of personal grooming, or make personal phone calls.

6. Try not to Interrupt

It's great to be friendly with your coworkers, but everyone has a job to do, so it can be irritating to be constantly pinged with e-mail forwards, bombarded by personal conversations, invited to look at pictures of someone's new baby, or deal with other non-business-related interruptions. People do tend to naturally socialize at certain times of the day—like first thing in the morning, during lunch, and at the end of the day—so try to bond with your team during these moments when people are most likely to be up for a conversation. Constant interruptions can make your coworkers view your adorable-animal videos as mere annoyances.

The office isn't so different from any other public space—if you exercise respect and discretion, there's no reason why everyone can't get along just fine. As long as you refrain from discussing last night's party at your desk, your coworker will be more likely to keep her cell phone quiet—in theory, that is. There will probably always be one person who scratches inappropriately and can't remember to get his dishes out of the sink, but as long as you follow these words of advice, at least it won't be you.

(By Allison Ford)

Unit 8   Socializing after Work

Learning Objectives

Social intercourse[1] is very important in international commercial activities. It can strengthen[2] the ties, promote the friendship between you and your counterparts[3] and deal with each other successfully. Social intercourse includes many activities, such as exchange of friendly visits, inviting to dinner, ballroom dancing and so on. From Kary's story, you will know that entertaining clients the right way is a positive way to establish and keep good business relationships.

Warming-up

1. When you have visitors (colleagues, customers, etc.), do you invite them out in the evening? If so, do you invite them to your home, to restaurant, or somewhere else? How formal are these occasions?

2. Toasting often marks the start of a social conversation. On which of the following occasions do you make toasts? Who or what do you toast?

—parties

—work celebrations

—drinks with friends

—dinner with business associates

—an informal lunch with colleagues

---

① intercourse 交往；交流

② strengthen 加强；变坚固

③ counterpart 同仁

Kary's Story

Dialogue 1 Invitation for the Dinner

(K = Kary, a Chinese businessperson; D = David Foss, a Danish engineer)

K: Hello, Mr. Foss. I wonder if you are free tomorrow evening?

D: I'm not sure, but let me check my schedule...Ah, no. I have nothing then.

K: Great! Our president has asked me to come over to invite you to the banquet[①] held in your honor at the Golden Hotel at 6:30. Here's an invitation card for you. And we'll have a dance party after the dinner.

D: How nice of him! Thanks for your invitation. I'll be delighted to go.

K: Please ask your wife to join us for dinner.

D: Thank you. It's very thoughtful of you. I think she would be glad to go with me.

K: Well, shall I pick you up at 6 o'clock then?

D: That's very nice of you, but won't it be too troublesome[②] for you?

K: No, no trouble at all. It's my pleasure. And there will be some other friends whom you will be glad to meet, I think.

D: That's great. I guess it will be the chance for me to know more business associates. I'm sure I'll enjoy their company.

K: Well, then, see you tomorrow.

► Useful sentences

1. Our president has asked me to come over to invite you to the banquet held in your honor...

我们董事长要我来请你参加……为你举办的宴会。

2. It's very thoughtful of you.

你想得可真周到。

3. I guess it will be the chance for me to know more business associates.

我想这是我结识更多生意伙伴的一个好机会。

► Other useful sentences

1. Are you free on Friday night?

周五晚上有空吗?

---

① banquet 宴会

② troublesome 令人讨厌的, 引起麻烦的

Do you have plans for Friday night?

周五晚上忙不忙？

Are you busy on Friday night?

周五晚上忙不忙？

Have you been occupied① on Friday night?

周五晚上有别的安排吗？

Will you have a lot of free time on Friday night?

周五晚上你有空闲时间吗？

2．Making invitation 发出邀请

Our General Manager wants to have dinner with you.

我们总经理想邀请您共进晚餐。

If it's convenient for you, we'd like to hold a party for you.

如果您方便的话，我们想为您举办一个聚会。

We'd be delighted as well as honored if you could come to our annual celebration tomorrow evening.

如果您能出席明晚举办的年度庆祝晚会，我们会很开心并且深感荣幸。

May we have the honor of having you as our guest?

我们能有幸邀请您担任嘉宾呢？

Wednesday's dinner has been arranged at the Hilton Hotel from 7 o'clock.

周三的晚宴已定在希尔顿酒店举行，从 7 点开始。

3．Accepting invitation 接受邀请

I'd be very happy /delighted / pleased to accept your invitation.

我很开心地接受你的邀请。

I'd very much like to accept your invitation.

我很乐意接受你的邀请。

It would give me the greatest pleasure to accept your invitation.

收到你的邀请，我深感荣幸。

---

① be occupied 被占用的，无暇抽身

Tips：

Writing and delivering invitations to customers to attend your important business-related occasions requires careful attention. A professional, attractive, and effective invitation will bring more guests. The following guidelines will help you make your business invitation letter or card professional and effective：

(1) Personal attention—start your invitation with the recipient's first name, i. e. "Dear George", instead of "Dear Madam or Sir ".

(2) Make it brief—a short, effective invitation answers these questions：What? Where? When?

(3) Be creative—use humor to make people smile.

(4) Set a convenient date.

(5) Deliver a printed invitation.

Dialogue 2　Talking at the Table

(K = Kary, a Chinese businessperson; W = Walter Barry, a Marketing Manager from UK)

K：This is your seat, Mr. Barry. Take your seat, please.

W：Thank you, Kary. I'm really a bit nervous now. I know little about Chinese food and your table manners. It would be in bad taste for a guest to make blunders[①].

K：Don't worry, Mr. Barry. Some people say that it's a great pity to leave China without doing three things—going to the Great Wall, eating Beijing Roast Duck and drinking Maotai. So tonight we are going to make the last two things come true.

W：Really? You have no idea how much I've been looking forward to a real Chinese meal.

K：I'm glad you enjoy Chinese food and hope the dishes will give you a better idea of Chinese cooking. As for table manners, there is only one rule to remember. That is making yourself at home.

W：No wonder people say the Chinese are hospitable[②]. Now, I have seen it with my own eyes. As the saying goes, "When in Rome, do as the Romans do." Although

---

① make blunders 犯错误

② hospitable 好客的；热情友好的

I am clumsy① with chopsticks，I like to learn to handle them.

K：Let me show you. Look，at first place both sticks between the thumb and the forefinger. Then，keep one still and move the other，so as to make them work like pincers②.

W：Let me try... Well，how is that?

K：Fine，you are learning fast，Mr. Barry. Well，to your health and success in business. Cheers.

W：And to yours. Cheers.

▶ Useful sentences

1．It would be in bad taste for a guest to make blunders.

如果客人失礼了，那就难堪了。

2．No wonder people say the Chinese are hospitable. Now，I have seen it with my own eyes.

难怪人们都说中国人好客。现在我算亲眼看到了。

3．Although I am clumsy with chopsticks，I like to learn to handle them.

尽管我用筷子有点笨拙，我想学会使用他们。

4．Then，keep one still and move the other，so as to make them work like pincers.

接着固定这根而移动另一根，这样就可以使他们像钳子一样灵活了。

▶ Other useful sentences

1．Make yourself at home 像在家一样不要客气。

Help yourself to whatever you like，Mr. Barry.

巴里先生，请随便吃，不用客气。

Don't stand on ceremony，Mr. Barry.

别太拘束，巴里先生。

Make yourself free，Mr. Barry.

巴里先生，不必拘礼。

Please enjoy yourself / feel free /go ahead，Mr. Barry.

巴里先生，玩得开心。/请尽情放松。/做你喜欢的事情。

2．Cheers! 干杯!

I propose a toast to our friendship!

我建议为我们的友谊举杯!

Let's drink to our everlasting friendship!

---

① clumsy 笨拙的；复杂难懂的

② pincer 钳子，镊子

为我们的友谊长存干杯!

To your health and success in your work / business.

为您身体健康、事业成功/生意兴隆干杯。

With great pleasure I ask you to toast the long-term cooperation between us.

我荣幸地请诸位为我们的长期合作干杯。

I ask you to join me in drinking to the future success of our cooperation.

请您跟我一起举杯预祝我们合作成功。

I drink for the future; may it bring us all happiness.

我为未来干杯,愿它给我们大家带来幸福。

Tips:

　　Most North Americans don't mind mixing business with pleasure, but this is not necessary true for other western cultures. This is especially true if part or all of your client entertainment involves dining. Some westerners prefer to discuss business before dining, some during, and some only after. If you're entertaining foreigners, be sure you have a good idea of their business practices!

Dialogue 3　At the Dance Party

(K = Kary, a Chinese businessperson; G = Goodman, the director of marketing department from USA)

　　K：Ladies and gentlemen, a dance party for welcoming Mr. Goodman is now beginning. I wish you would enjoy yourselves.

　　G：Thank you for giving the dance party, Kary. I think I'll have good time with all the friends here.

　　K：Now the music is going on. Please enjoy yourselves!

　　G：Can you oblige me with a social dance①, Kary?

　　K：With pleasure. I think you dance much.

　　G：Oh, no, to tell you the truth, I have not danced for a long time.

　　K：Because of business, I have not danced for a long time, either.

　　G：Still you dance wonderfully well.

　　K：Thanks. I'm glad you say so.

　　G：How do you spend your weekend when you are in your country?

---

①　oblige sb. with sth. 便满足,答应某人的请求

K：We have many recreational activities①. Sometimes we go to the movies. Sometimes we go to concerts. Young people like music and dancing, and they spend much time at the nightclub. Older people usually settle for② the game of bridge. What recreational activities do you like best?

G：I like playing golf. My wife is an avid movie-fan. Sometimes we all go to dance. We also go in for③ amateur photography④.

K：The music stopped. Let's go to the buffet⑤ and get something to drink.

G：Great！It is a nice time to dance with you. Thank you.

▶ Useful sentences

1. Can you oblige me with a social dance?

你能赏光和我跳个舞吗?

Will you accept my arm?

请你跳个舞好吗?

Will you favor me with a dance?

你愿意和我跳个舞吗?

Will you honor me with a dance?

请你赏光和我跳个舞好吗?

May I have the honor of a dance?

可以赏光和我跳个舞吗?

2. to tell you the truth 说实话

3. go in for 从事；喜欢

We also go in for amateur photography. 我们还都爱好业余摄影。

▶ Other useful sentences

1. First，let's have a look on a game of volleyball，then go to dance. In the evening I'll accompany you to the theatre.

我们先看一场排球比赛，再去跳舞，晚上我再陪你去看戏。

2. After dinner，I accompany you to go to the National Theatre seeing a Beijing Opera, which is Chinese traditional opera.

晚饭以后，我陪你去国家剧院看京剧，这是中国传统的戏剧。

----

① recreational activities 娱乐活动

② settle for 满足于

③ go in for 从事；喜欢

④ amateur photography 业余摄影

⑤ buffet 饮食柜台；快餐部；自助餐

107

3. I prefer waltzing and disco dancing, because those dances make me relaxed and free.

我更喜欢跳华尔兹和迪斯科，那些舞轻松、自由。

4. I like sports very much. And I enjoy playing basketball, football, especially golf. Do you know some golf courses nearby?

我很喜欢体育运动，比如说篮球、足球，尤其是高尔夫球。你知道附近有哪些高尔夫球场吗？

5. That's great! I like golf, too. And I know there is a nice golf course near our company where we can enjoy ourselves.

太好了！我也喜欢高尔夫球。我知道我们公司附近有一个不错的高尔夫球场，我们一定会在那儿玩得很开心的。

Listening Practice

1. **Listen to the recording of two short extracts, where hosts invite their visitors to take part in a social activity. The invitations are rejected.**

a) Identify each suggested activity.

b) Give the reasons for each rejection.

c) Do you think each rejection is appropriate? Explain your answers.

Activity (a)	Reason for rejection (b)	Comments (c)

2. **You will hear a short conversation about entertaining a client. In blanks 1 ~ 5, you should fill in a word or phrase, and in blanks 6 ~ 10, a sentence. Listen and fill in the blanks with the missing words or sentences.**

Entertaining a Client

Corporate hospitality _____ (1) the ways in which companies entertain their customers _____ (2) gain business. Entertaining clients or customers is quite common in the business world. Companies treat their clients to _____ (3), _____ ____ (4), _____ (5) in order to bring up the matter of business in a social setting.

Social events like these can not only make business talk easier, but also help further develop relationships with the clients. But, of course, entertaining clients at random① can be a waste of both time and money. _____ (6). First of all, you should be clear about what business objectives you want to achieve. This may help you decide on the right form of entertainment. You can not possibly have any intimate discussions while watching a football game. Second, _____ (7). If you treat your client to something he or she dislikes, you are certainly wasting your money! _____ (8). Although it is the company that covers all the expenses, you still have to be economical. A successful entertainment is one that __ _____ (9) and _____ (10).

Culture Note

The Importance of Socializing

In most cultures the business day hardly ends at 5 p.m. In fact, in many cultures outside of North America, sundown signals the start of "serious" relationship-building time—essential to the successful completion of business. The social occasion is often more important than the formal business meeting earlier in the day when it comes to closing a deal②. It's not so much that actual details of the business at hand will be discussed but rather relationships will be reinforced③.

Many cultures, however, are less subtle④ about the course of their business meals. In the United States, it is not considered rude to deal with specifics of the deal at mealtime. American attitudes towards mixing business with pleasure are relaxed. After all, the power breakfast is not meant to be a social occasion; It is a way of squeezing a few more hours of precious time out of the working day.

Work Hard, Play Hard

Regardless of the country you are in, it is essential to accept any invitation to meet outside of business hours. Pleading jetlag, lack of hunger, illness or alcoholic abstinence can be insults to a host and are more often than not taken as signs of smugness⑤ and

---

① random 任意的；随机的

② come to closing a deal 达成交易

③ be reinforced 加固；加强

④ subtle 微妙敏感的

⑤ smugness 装模作样；骄矜

superiority[1]. Deprived of this relationship-building time, it would be difficult to imagine business moving ahead at all in certain cultures.

Of course, mealtimes vary in different cultures. Do your homework and learn the times when everyone eats and plan accordingly. In many Latin cultures (almost all of Latin America, Italy and Spain) as well as the Middle East, lunch is the main meal of the day—and the meal where business relationships can be cemented. Tanking up at the breakfast buffet may leave you stuffed for lunchtime just when you need to be impressing your foreign colleagues over a seven-course luncheon. Plan ahead. Eat a light breakfast instead—and remember that supper in countries where lunch is king is often very late in the evening and also a very light meal.

Dining Trepidation

If you travel, sooner or later you will be faced with the choice of trying some exotic[2] dish that may on the surface sound or look repulsive[3]. Most business people have a story connected with the first time they tried dog in Korea or sheep's eyes in Saudi Arabia or hot dogs covered in chili in the United States or hippos teaks in South Africa. Remember, rejection of such food is tantamount to rejection of your host's culture and country. Sometimes there is simply no way out and it is necessary to "take one for the team", as the Americans would say. One way to cope is to simply remain ignorant. Don't ask too many questions about what you are eating—simply try and enjoy it. If the food looks absolutely awful to you, try swallowing very small bites quickly—you probably won't even taste it. The revulsion[4] people feel about certain food is probably 95 percent mental. Crocodile does indeed taste like chicken—and often so do many other strange meats. And who knows, if

---

① superiority 优越（性），优等

② exotic 外来的；异国的

③ repulsive 令人厌恶的；排斥的

④ revulsion 剧变；非常的厌恶

you can get over your own culturally generated mental picture of what you are eating, you may even like the taste.

Pair Work

▶ Task 1

Complete the following dialogues in pairs and practise it.

1. A：Our manager would like to invite you to a dinner party this evening.

   B：_____. （太好了，我很乐意去。）

2. A：If you are free, please come and join us !

   B：_____. （很遗憾地告诉你，因已有约，不能前往赴宴。）

3. A：The banquet will begin at 6：00 p. m. We'll arrange a car to meet you at your hotel at 5：30 p. m. Please wait for me in front of the hotel gate.

   B：_____. （谢谢你。你真好。我一定在旅馆门前等你。）

4. A：Now, Mr. B, dinner is ready. Let's go into the dining hall. Ladies and gentlemen, please be seated. Mr. B, will you please sit on left?

   B：_____. （非常感谢你的邀请。我一直听人们说中国人很好客，这回我算是亲眼所见了。）

5. A：It is the 15th anniversary of our company today. As the host, I want to propose a toast to all present. The success of this company should be owed to all of you. I want to take this opportunity to say：Thank you. Please raise your glasses. To your health, to our friendship and cooperation. Bottoms up !

   B：_____. （为所有在座的人的健康，为我们的友谊和合作，干杯!）

6. A：I don't want to baby-feed you, you know. So please feel free and help yourself to anything you like.

   B：_____. （谢谢，你不要替我担心，我什么菜都不会错过。）

7. A：It is the weekend today. We are having a dance party. I hope everybody enjoys yourself.

   B：_____. （A 先生，谢谢您举行这次舞会，我想我们一定会过得愉快的。）

8. A：How do you usually spend your weekend, Mr. B?

   B：_____. （哦，我们有许多文娱活动，有时我们去看电影，有时为我们去听音乐，年轻人喜欢流行歌曲和跳舞，我常打高尔夫球。)

9. A：Thank you for the wonderful evening.

   B：_____. (我很高兴你今晚玩得愉快。欢迎下次再来参加我们的舞会。)

▶ Task 2

Discuss with each other and design a scene, and organize a suitable dialogue by imitate some of the drills above and act it out.

Socializing Practice

▶ Role-play

Use the following described situation to construct a dialogue. Prepare your role and then act it out.

Student A：

You are Susan, the secretary from company A in Shanghai. Your boss, Michael, had invited Mr. Smith, who is from company B in Tianjin, to have dinner tonight. But due to some unexpected reasons, the arrangement has to be changed. You are trying to inform Mr. Smith from company B.

Student B：

You are Mr. Smith, the director of company B in Tianjin. You had Michael's invitation for tonight's dinner yesterday. But his secretary tells you that the dinner time has to be changed because of some unexpected reasons. You agreed on it.

Daily Practice

▶ Tongue twister

1. How can a clam cram in a clean cream can?

一只蛤蟆怎么可以塞满干净的奶油罐头！

2. Susan shines shoes and socks; she ceased shining shoes and socks for shoes and socks shock Susan.

苏珊把鞋子和袜子擦亮，她停止了将鞋子和袜子擦亮，因为鞋子和袜子把苏珊吓坏了。

3. I wish to wish the wish you wish to wish, but if you wish the wish the witch wishes, I won't wish the wish you wish to wish.

我想许你想许的愿望，但是如果你许的是女巫的愿望，我不会许你想许的愿望。

4. A pleasant peasant keeps a pleasant pheasant and both the peasant and the pheasant are having a pleasant time together.

一个快乐的农夫养了一只伶俐的野鸡，农民和这只伶俐的野鸡在一起度过了快乐的时光。

▶ Read aloud

You Have Only One Life

There are moments in life when you miss someone so much that you just want to pick them from your dreams and hug them for real! Dream what you want to dream; go where you want to go; be what you want to be, because you have only one life and one chance to do all the things you want to do.

May you have enough happiness to make you sweet, enough trails to make you strong, enough sorrow to keep you human, enough hope to make you happy. Always put yourself in other's shoes. If you feel that it hurts you, it probably hurts the other person, too.

The happiest people don't necessarily have the best of everything; they just make the most of everything that comes along their way. Happiness lies for those who cry, those who hurt, those who have searched, and those who have tried, for only they can appreciate the importance of people who have touched their lives. Love begins with a smile, grows with a kiss and ends with a tear. The brightest future will always be based on a forgotten past, and you can't go on well in life until you let go of your past failures and heartaches.

When you were born, you were crying and everyone around you was smiling. Live your life so that when you die, you're the one who is smiling and everyone around you is crying.

Please send this message to those people who mean something to you, to those who have touched your life in one way or another, to those who make you smile when you feel really need it, to those that make you see the brighter side of things when you feel really down, to those who you want to let them know that you appreciate their friendships. And if you don't, don't worry, nothing bad will happen to you, and you will just miss out on the opportunity to brighten someone's day with this message.

Unit 9　Non-verbal Communication

Learning Objectives

Kary is going to learn some knowledge on body language and other non-verbal behaviours of different cultures around the world. Kary's objectives are to master the basic words, expressions and useful sentences of non-verbal communication; to learn the skills of using proper body language to communicate with customers or other people during the work. Kary's experiences will help you to understand the significance and know the different ways of nonverbal communication around the world and give some tips to deal with the practical problems and avoid misunderstanding during your business.

Warming-up

1.　Do you know what the following gestures mean?

2. What are the contents of non-verbal communication?Tick（√）the box.

（　）job

（　）hair

（　）smile

（　）gesture

（　）perfume

（　）dressing

（　）nationality

（　）appearance

（　）eye-contact

（　）color of skin

（　）facial expressions

（　）distance between each other

3. Test your cross-cultural knowledge，using "T"（true）or "F"（false）.

（　）American people like keeping the time.

（　）African and Arab people have a flexible attitude[①] to time.

（　）People of Saudi Arabia like to stand closer to their business partners.

（　）Nodding the head means I agree in Japanese culture.

（　）Thumbs-up means "good" in most of the world but it means "Number Five" in Germany.

（　）Shrugging one's shoulders[②] means "I don't know" in the US.

Kary's Story

With the rapid expansion of company's business，Kary has chance to meet the customers of many regions and countries. She finds it interesting that people from different places have their special cultures，such as the body language，gesture，and the distances and wants to know more in this field. Therefore Kary learns the knowledge of non-verbal communication from the experienced colleague and attends the internal lecture of her company.

（K = Kary；M = Michelle，Kary's colleague）

---

① flexible attitude 灵活的态度

② shrugging one's shoulders 耸肩

Dialogue 1 Meeting a Woman from Japan

K：Michelle, do you know much about body language in countries around the world?

M：Sure. I've picked up a few things from travelling around for work. What do you want to know?

K：Well, I had a meeting today with a woman from Japan and she wouldn't stop bowing! I didn't know what to do!

M：Did you bow back?

K：No, I tried to shake her hand, but her hand was so limp. I was a bit offended.

M：Well, Japanese businessmen and women typically① bow to greet each other in Japan. She might have been offended by your strong handshake.

K：But she was in China! Shouldn't she have known that strong handshakes in China signify confidence and respect?

M：Things are different in Japan. You know, in some countries, making eye contact with others is considered rude.

K：Is that why she wouldn't look at me in the meeting?

M：I think it's highly possible.

K：The meeting really didn't go down well at all. I think I need to read up about intercultural communication before I have another meeting with someone from another country.

M：That's a good idea. When you don't know much about other cultures, the simpliest thing can offend someone.

K：That's so true. It's great that we see eye to eye on this.

▶▶ Useful sentences

1. I have picked up a few things from travelling around for work.

我曾到不同国家出差，对它们的肢体语言有一定的了解。

2. She wouldn't stop bowing!

她不停地鞠躬。

3. I tried to shake her hand, but her hand was so limp. I was a bit offended.

我尝试和她握手，但她的手软弱无力。我感觉有点生气。

4. Shouldn't she have known that strong handshakes in China signify confidence and respect?

———————

① typically 通常地，典型地

116

难道她不知道在中国用力握手意味着自信和尊重对方吗？

5. I think I need to read up about intercultural communication before I have another meeting with someone from another country.

在会见来自其他国家的客户之前，我认为还是有必要去弄懂跨文化交流这方面的知识。

6. It's great that we see eye to eye on this.

我们在这个问题上能有相同的见解实在太棒了。

▶ Other useful sentences

1. Non-verbal communication 非言语交际

Non-verbal communication is the process of communication through sending and receiving wordless cues between people.

非言语交流就是人们通过发出或接收非言语的信息进行交流。

2. The meanings of smile 笑容的含义

In most parts of the world, the meaning of smile is to show your friendliness and politeness. But in some cultures, smile has some other meanings. In America, a smile also expresses happiness or friendly affirmation while in Japan, smile is a way to avoid embarrassment and unpleasantness.

在大多数国家和地区，微笑意味着向他人示好和表示礼貌。但在某些文化里，微笑也有其他的含义。如在美国，微笑可以表示开心或者善意的肯定；而在日本，微笑也许是避免尴尬或者掩饰悲伤的一种方式。

3. The gestures of greeting others 与他人打招呼的姿势

Two kinds of gestures of greeting others are widely used all over the world: nodding head and waving hands.

点头与握手是世界上两种常见的用于互相问候的身势语。

4. The way of farewell 告别的方式

Waving hands is a universal way to farewell each other, but some people put their fingers close to the ear when they say "goodbye", which means "keep contact in the future".

挥手是告别的一种常用的方式，然而有些人在告别的时候把手指贴在耳边，意思是"以后常联系"。

Tips：

Pay more attention to your non-verbal behaviours when you are meeting your clients or business partners. Here are some tips.

1. Dress appropriately and neatly and match your clothes harmoniously.
穿着整洁得体，衣服搭配协调。

2. We greet people in different ways according to their cultures. If your clients or business partners are American women, it is better to let her hand first. If she has no intention of shaking hands, we may nod or bow to her.

我们应视对方的文化打招呼。如果是来自美国的女性客户，握手时应等其先伸出手。如果她无握手之意，则只需要点头或者鞠躬即可。

3. Embracing is an important and popular way to greet each other in western culture. If you are not used to it, don't be nervous. Just stretch out your right hand.

在西方文化中，拥抱是一种重要且流行的打招呼方式。如果你不习惯的话，不必惊慌失措，只需伸出右手即可。

4. Strong fragrances are unadvisable in the presence of customers, along with garlic and cigarette breath.

见客户时香水不宜擦太浓，也要避免有大蒜和香烟口气。

Dialogue 2   A Course on Body Language

In this dialogue, Royce is telling Kary all about a course on body language that she went on.

(K = Kary; R = Royce, Kary's colleague)

R: I've just finished the course on body language.

K: It is interesting and useful?

R: Yes, it was really interesting and I learnt all sorts of useful things.

K: I am curious about the knowledge of body language. Please tell me something about it.

R: Well, if someone touches his nose while he is talking, it's a sign that he's lying.

K: How about the sign of biting nails?

R: People bite nails means that they are nervous or worried about something.

K: Any other interesting things?

R: If people fold their arms across their chests, it means they feel threatened and they are being offended.

K: It sounds reasonable.

R: If someone leans forward, it means he is interested. And if he leans back in his chair, it means he is feeling very relaxed and confident.

K: That's really something new to me. I think there are so many things to learn from body language.

R: You are right, body language is also an important way to express yourself, so sometimes we should care our behaviours and try to give a good impression to others.

K: Thanks a lot. I am glad to learn this from you.

▶ Useful sentences

1. I am curious about the knowledge of body language.

我对身势语言的知识感到很好奇。

2. If people fold their arms across their chests, it means they feel threatened and they are being offended.

如果人们交叉双臂放在胸前，意味着他们感受到威胁和处于被冒犯的状态。

3. If someone leans forward, it means he is interested.

如果某人朝前探过身子，则意味着他对某事较感兴趣。

4. Body language is also an important way to express yourself.

肢体语言也是表达自己想法的一种重要方式。

Dialogue 3   A Lecture on Personal Distance

There is an internal lecture on the distance among people from different areas. Kary is interested and attends the lecture given by her colleague who often has meeting and negotiates with foreigners. The followings are the content of the lecture.

Dear colleagues, I am glad to give a lecture on the distance among people. From the result of some researches on distance, we can see that there are four major types of distances in our social and business circumstances.

The first type of distance is the intimate[①] distance. It is about 0cm to 45cm. Of all the distances, intimate distance is the most important one. People who have very close relationships with the person such as his/her lover, parents, spouse and children are allowed to keep such a close distance. And the most intimate distance is within 15cm. People are not supposed to enter this distance unless there is going to be some body contact. The second type of distance is the personal distance. It is about 46cm to 122cm. People keep this distance when they are at some parties or in other situations with their friends, relatives or acquaintances[②]. The third type is the social distance, ranging from 123cm to 360cm. This is for people who work together, or people doing business, as well as most of

---

① intimate 亲密的

② relative or acquaintance 亲戚或熟人

119

those in conversation at social gatherings①. The last type is the public distance. It is farther than 3. 6 meters and it is usually for speakers in public and for teachers in classrooms. People at lectures, concerts, plays, speeches and ceremonies take this kind of distance.

What I have talked above is mostly suitable for the people who live in Australia, New Zealand, England, North America and Canada. That is to say, the standards for these four kinds of space differ from culture to culture and from person to person. For example, people from colder climates generally use large physical distances during their communication and those from warm climates prefer close distances.

So much are the four types of distances we often use during our daily life, work or business. I hope this knowledge will be helpful for each of you. Thank you for your attention!

▶ Useful sentences

1. We can see that there are four major types of distances in our social and business circumstances.

我们可以得知在社交与商业场合有四种不同的距离。

2. People are not supposed to enter this distance unless there is going to be some body contact.

如果接下来不是有身体接触的话，人们一般不会靠得如此之近。

3. The third type is the social distance, ranging from 123cm to 360cm.

第三种是社交场合的距离，从 123 厘米到 360 厘米不等。

4. People at lectures, concerts, plays, speeches and ceremonies take this kind of distance.

人们在听讲座、欣赏音乐会、看戏剧、出席演讲致辞和参加庆典时会采用这样的距离。

5. That is to say, the standards for these four kinds of space differ from culture to culture and from person to person.

也就是说，上述四种类型的距离的标准会随着文化与个体的差异而有所不同。

6. People from colder climates generally use large physical distances during their communication.

来自寒冷气候的人在与他人进行言语交流时通常会保持较大的距离。

🔘 Listening Practice

You are going to listen to a passage about body language and finish task A and B.

---

① social gathering 社交聚会

Task A: **Decide which of these statements are true （T）and which are false （F）. If the statement is false, explain why it is wrong.**

（　）1. Body language is always as important as spoken language.

（　）2. If you want to show your friendliness, you may smile to others.

（　）3. If you sit looking away from a person, or with your back turned, you may be protecting yourself from a talk you do not want.

（　）4. You should not greet your new boss by giving him or her a hug.

（　）5. Body language is mostly the same all over the world.

Task B: **Listen again and finish the following sentences.**

1. In most countries, ＿＿＿＿＿＿＿＿＿＿＿＿shows agreement.

2. You ＿＿＿＿＿＿＿＿＿your boss or teacher and should stand with ＿＿＿＿＿＿＿＿.

3. ＿＿＿＿＿＿＿＿＿countries, children are taught that looking directly at an adult is not a good behaviour.

Culture Note

Types of Non-verbal Communication

There are mainly three types of non-verbal communication.

1. Body Language

Body language includes gestures, head movements, facial expressions, eye behaviours, postures and other displays that can be used to communicate. Some body language signals may have special meanings in a particular society. Here are some tips for you to avoid misunderstanding when communicating with people from different cultures.

1）Nodding the head means "Yes" in most societies, but it means "No" in some parts of Greece, Bulgaria[①] and Turkey.

2）Eye contact is encouraged in America, Canada and Europe, but it's considered to be rude in most Asian countries and in Africa.

3）The signal "OK" (the thumb and forefinger form a circle) means "fine" or "OK" in most cultures, but it means "zero" or "worthless" in some parts of Europe. You should notice that it's an insult signal[②] in Greece, Brazil, Italy, Turkey and Russia.

4）Pointing with the index finger is common in North America and Europe. But it is considered impolite in Japan where people favor using the whole open hand.

5）In Asia and some European countries, putting feet up on a desk or any other piece of

---

① Bulgaria 保加利亚

② insult signal 侮辱性质的行为

121

furniture is very disrespectful①. And sitting cross-legged, while common in North America and some European countries, is very impolite in other parts of the world.

2. Paralanguage

1) Pitch.

When one is excited, his/her voice would be high in pitch, quick in rate, and there will be no pauses between sentences. When one is sad or depressed, his/her voice traits would surely be the opposite.

2) Volume.

The English speak in lower voice when they make speech or a lecture, or talking with each other, or phoning, while Chinese incline to speak in louder voice in the above occasions. Americans are more skilled in regulating② their voice volume and use many different volume levels depending on the size of the audience and the physical environment.

3) Silence.

American consider keeping silence means disagreement while Chinese and Japanese's keeping silence suggests that they need more time to think over before making a decision.

People of English-speaking countries are not fond of adopting silent way in business affairs. They consider this is impolite and disrespectful to their business partners. And they consider keeping silence means disagreement. But Asian people such as Chinese and Japanese prefer keeping silence during business negotiation when they need more time to think over before making decisions. To Chinese and Japanese, silence also means acquiescence and approval③ for the bargain.

3. Environment Language

1) Space.

It refers to the body distance which is divided into short, medium and long distance. People from different cultures keep different types of body distance.

Short	Mediterranean Europeans Mediterranean Arabs Latins
Medium	Northern Europeans Americans
Long	Japanese

---

① disrespectful 无礼的

② regulate 调节

③ acquiescence and approval 默许与赞成

2）Time.

There are two time systems: Monochronic Time (M-Time) and Polychronic Time (P-Time).

Northern American, Western and Northern European cultures are typical M-Time cultures. The two striking features of M-Time are punctuality and promptness①. Latin American, African, Arab and most Asian cultures are P-Time cultures. They schedule several activities at the same time and the time is more flexible and more human-centered.

Pair Work

1. Take turn to be the representative② of Great Britain, France, Japan, Jordan and China. Try to find the answer to the question: How do you greet each other and what about the physical distance in your country?

1）If you are from Britain, how do you greet each other and what about the physical distance?

2）If you are from France, ...

3）If you are from Japan, ...

4）If you are from Jordan, ...

5）If you are from China, ...

2. Choose one of the following situations to act out, using the proper body language to help you.

1）You meet the business partner at the airport and talk to each other.

2）You try to show someone the way in the street.

3）You see a friend in the distance and greet him/her.

4）You enter a friend's house and talk with him/her.

5）You fall and hurt your foot while you are hiking on a lonely path. You need help, and see someone in the distance.

6）You are visiting a strange city and need to buy some water and oranges. You only know a little English and want to know where you can get them and how much they cost.

---

① punctuality and promptness 准时且迅速

② representative 代表

Socializing Practice

Role-play

At a local real estate agent's office, Alan is behind the customer service counter. He is on the phone dealing with a difficult inquiry[①] when a customer approaches[②] the counter. He keeps talking on the phone and when the customer says, "Excuse me." He does not look up but holds a hand up with one finger extended, indicating that he'll be one minute.

Task 1: Question for all students: What body language should you use towards a customer, when on the phone?

Task 2 (for student A): Suppose you are Alan's supervisor[③], what would you say to him about the body language and managing his responsibilities[④] for greeting customers both on the phone and face to face?

Task 3 (for student B): Imagine that you are the customer. When you enter the office, the customer service receptionist is on the phone. You wait. You try to get his attention but he holds up his hand with a finger. How do you feel?

Task 4: Discussion on "What should the clerk (Alan) have done differently to ensure that all of his customers are taken care of?"

Discussion

What kinds of jobs incline to use a lot of non-verbal communication? Make a brief introduction on it. The example is given as follow:

Body language is rather important for the work of traffic police. They use a lot of gestures to guide the vehicles[⑤] to move orderly. For example, when a traffic police raises his left hand at 135 degree, it's a sign of stop moving all the cars. When he raises his right hand at 45 degree, it means that you must slow down and stop your car by the roadside[⑥].

Assignment after class

Surf the Internet and tell the meanings for the following pictures.

----

① inquiry 询问
② approach 走进，靠近
③ supervisor 主管
④ manage one's responsibility 尽自己的责任
⑤ vehicle 机动车辆
⑥ by the roadside 停在路旁

Daily Practice

▶ Tongue twister

1. If two witches would watch two watches, which witch would watch which watch?

如果两个巫婆看管两块表，到底哪个巫婆会看管哪块表呢？

2. A Finnish fisher named Fisher failed to fish any fish one Friday afternoon and finally he found out a big fissure in his fishing net.

一个名叫费希尔的芬兰渔民在一个星期五的下午未能捕捉到任何鱼，后来他发现他的渔网上有一个大裂口。

3. How many cookies could a good cook cook if a good cook could cook cookies? A good cook could cook as many cookies as a good cook who could cook cookies.

如果一个好的厨师能做小甜饼，那么他能做多少小甜饼呢？一个好的厨师能做出和其他好厨师一样多的小甜饼。

4. She sells seashells on the seashore, and the shells she sells are seashells, I am sure. If she sells shells at the seashore, the shells she sells are seashells for sure.

她在海边卖海贝壳，我确定她卖的贝类是海贝壳。如果她是在海边卖贝壳，那么她卖的贝类肯定是海贝壳。

5. A flea and a fly flew up in a flue. Said the flea, "Let us fly!" Said the fly, "Let us flee!" So they flew through a flaw in the flue.

一只跳蚤和一只苍蝇飞进烟道里。跳蚤说："让我们飞吧！"苍蝇说："让我们逃跑吧！"就这样，它们飞越了烟道里的一条裂纹。

▶ Read aloud

Throughout the history of mankind, people have communicated with body language. In many situations, the way you say something is far more important than what you say. The open hand and eye contact are two universal signs of non-verbal communication.

What will people do if they are meeting a stranger in an unfamiliar place? Sometimes people are dangerous and humans have to find ways to protect themselves. They have to make sure they can trust others they do not know and have to show that they are not dangerous as well. The open hand is a sign used to weaken the feeling of hostility because showing your hands means that you are not armed. In many cultures today, the western custom of shaking hands is used. People use their right hands, which are usually stronger than the left ones. If they are using hands this way, it cannot be holding a knife or a gun. It shows that they can trust the other person, and that the other person also can trust them.

Eye contact is sometimes the key to communication. It can signal friendliness or hostility, interest or boredom, and understanding or confusion. In western cultures, maintaining eye contact in conversations is necessary. As a matter of fact, a westerner might consider a lack of eye contact as a lack of interest. In Spain, Italy and Greece, where people stand close together talking to each other, eye contact is more frequent and lasts longer. In many Asian cultures, avoiding eye contact shows respect. It is done when talking with anyone in authority or with anyone older. Habits like this can cause problems when people from other cultures do not understand them. For instance, an Asian might close his eyes in concentration or look down while listening to a speaker. A western speaker might think the man is not interested.

It is an amusing thing to explore the origins of all sorts of body language and to find out the differences among different cultures.

Unit 10   Making Farewells

Learning Objectives

In international commercial activities, it's necessary to reserve hotel rooms for the guests. When the guests leave, it's good manners for you to see them off in person, or at least, to send a representative to see them off. Mr. Smith has succeeded in concluding the business with Kary, and will set up a joint venture in China. His visiting China has achieved a lot. Now he has got ready to leave China and return to America. Before Mr. Brown's departure, Kary holds a homely dinner[①] for him. The next day, Kary sees him off at the airport. Kary's story will guide you to learn how to see off customers properly and politely.

Warming-up

1. How do you behave when you say goodbye to:

—your parents?

—a friend?

—a visitor who is returning to his/her country after a five-day visit?

—a colleague who is leaving to take up a promotion in another part of the company?

2. Make a short response to each of the following farewell wishes.

(1) Enjoy your holiday.

(2) See you soon.

(3) Have a good weekend.

(4) I hope the sea stays calm for the crossing.

(5) Drive carefully.

---

①   a homely dinner 家宴 ·

Kary's Story

Dialogue 1　Giving a Farewell Homely Dinner

（K = Kary，a Chinese businessperson；S = Mr. Smith，an American businessman）

K：Good evening，Mr. Smith.

S：Good evening，Kary. Thank you for giving me a homely dinner.

K：We are very honored by your presence at the dinner. Now，let's be seated. Have a cup of tea，please.

S：Thank you. I like Chinese tea very much.

K：I'm glad to hear that.

S：Here are some American picture books for your daughter. I'd like you to accept them as a token① of my gratitude for all your help.

K：What lovely books they are！They will always remind me of you②，the old friend of ours. Thank you，Mr. Smith. Now，dinner is ready. Mr. Smith，please go to the table.

S：The dishes look so tempting③. I think Chinese food is the best of the world.

K：I'm glad you like it. Our Chinese cuisine takes care of color，flavor and taste. Help yourself，please！

S：Thank you. Kary，what do we say in Chinese for "Bottoms up"？

K：We say "Gan bei". I wish to propose a toast to our friendship and cooperation. Gan bei！

S：To our friendship and cooperation. Gan bei！

▶ Useful sentences

1. Thank you for giving me a homely dinner.

非常感谢你邀请我来参加家宴。

2. We are very honored by your presence at the dinner.

你出席我们的薄宴，我们十分高兴。

3. I'd like you to accept them as a token of my gratitude for all your help.

但愿笑纳，以表谢意。

---

① token 象征；标志

② remind sb. of sth. 使某人想起某物

③ tempting 诱惑人的

4. Our Chinese cuisine takes care of color, flavor and taste.

中国烹饪注重色、香、味俱全。

▶▶ Other useful sentences

1. Mr. Black invites me to have dinner with his family during my staying in Britain. What an appropriate gift should I bring with me?

在出差英国期间，布莱克先生邀请我去他家吃饭，我该带什么礼物去才合适呢？

2. If you really want to bring something, it should be a small inexpensive item. You could bring some candy or toys for the kids or something special from China. But better not the things on which printed your company's name for personal friends.

如果你真想带礼物的话，它应该是一件小而廉价的东西。你可以给小孩子带一包糖、一个玩具或是从中国带去的什么特产。但最好不要送带有你自己公司名字的东西作为私人礼物。

3. We think the idea is to bring a nice "token" gift that says "I thought of you", not a gift that says "Look, how much money I spent".

我们认为带一个有象征意义的礼物是表明"我想着你"，而不是用一个礼物去表明"看，我花了多少钱"。

4. Please accept this gift. It's a token of our friendship.

请收下这份礼物，它是我们友谊的象征。

Dialogue 2　Say Goodbye over the Phone

(B = Betty, the marketing manager, Kary's boss; S = Mr. Smith, an American businessman)

B：Hello, Mr. Smith. I am Betty.

S：Hi, Miss Betty. I am very glad that we have successfully signed the contract. I am going back tonight and I am just packing.

B：Oh, sorry to interrupt you. But I am calling to say goodbye to you. I am awfully sorry to tell you that I am afraid I could not see you off at the airport tonight, because I will have to attend a very important meeting.

S：It doesn't matter, Miss Betty. I can understand. I know you are always very busy. Work must come first.

B：Thanks a lot. You have been here for almost five days. How fast time flies!

S：Yes. And I would like to convey① my thanks to you and your company for your help

---

① convey 表达，转达

during my stay here in Guangzhou.

B：It is our pleasure. It has been a great pleasure to work with you.

S：Me too. I am looking forward to cooperating with you again.

B：Great! We will. Well, what's your flight number? When are you leaving tonight?

S：It's flight No. 258, Eastern Airlines, which leaves at ten o'clock tonight.

B：OK. Please take care and have a nice trip.

S：Thanks a lot. I am very pleased that our cooperation ends in not only a great success but also a friendship. I will be welcoming and looking forward to your visit.

B：Let's call it a deal①. Hope to see you again soon. Keep in touch then. Bye-bye.

S：Goodbye. Thanks again.

▶ Useful sentences

1. And I would like to convey my thanks to you and your company for your help during my stay here in Guangzhou.

在此我要向您和贵公司为我在广州期间所做的一切致以深深的感谢。

2. Please take care and have a nice trip.

您多保重，一路顺风。

3. Keep in touch then.

常联系。

Dialogue 3   Seeing off at the Airport

(K = Kary, a Chinese businessperson; S = Mr. Smith, an American businessman)

K：I'm sorry that you'll leave soon.

S：I wish I could stay a little longer, but I have lots to do back home, you know. I'd like to say it has been a very pleasant and productive② trip for me. Your company has left me a very good impression, and I am deeply moved by your hospitality. I think our cooperation will be a very successful one.

K：Thank you very much, Mr. Smith. We are looking forward to your reply.

---

① deal 协定；交易

② productive 富有成效的；有益的

S：OK, Kary. I will try my best to promote this transaction. Thank you very much for coming to the airport to see us off.

K：It's a pity that you haven't got the time to visit all the places of interest.

S：Business trip never leave much time for sightseeing.

K：Perhaps we can make things up next time you come here.

S：I hope so. I think we will have opportunities to meet each other in the future. Hope some day you will come to America for a visit.

K：Thank you. I will if I have chance. OK. I think it's time for you to check in. We wish you a safe and pleasant journey home.

S：Thank you. Bye-bye.

▶ Useful sentences

1. I wish I could stay a little longer, but I have lots to do back home, you know.
我希望能多待一些时间，但是你知道，国内还有很多工作要做。

2. I'd like to say it has been a very pleasant and productive trip for me.
我想说的是这次旅行让我感到很高兴并且收获颇丰。

3. Your company has left me a very good impression, and I am deeply moved by your hospitality.
贵公司给我留下了很好的印象，你们的热情好客让我深深感动。

4. Business trip never leave much time for sightseeing.
因公出差从来没有很多时间可以去观光。

5. Perhaps we can make things up next time you come here.
也许下次你来这儿，我们可以加以弥补。

▶ Other useful sentences

1. Now, you are to board the plane. We're sorry that we haven't done much to help you when you stayed in China.
现在你要登机了，很抱歉，你在中国的时候对你帮助得很不够。

2. I appreciate what you have done for me very much. Everything I have seen here has left a deep impression on me. I really don't know how to express my thanks to you.
十分感谢你对我的关照，在中国见到的一切给我留下了深刻的印象。我真不知怎样感谢你们。

3. At parting with you, we express deep regret and wish you a pleasant journey home. We hope you will come and join us again next year.
我们怀着不舍的心情送别你们。祝你们回家途中一路平安，希望你们明年再来。

4. At the moment of your departure, I take the greatest possible pleasure in sending you, on behalf of the department staff and in my own name, our best wishes.

临行之时，我极为愉快地代表本部全体成员，并以我个人的名义，向你们表示最美好的祝愿 。

Listening Practice

1. **Put yourself in the position of a visitor leaving after a short stay. Listen to these remarks made by your new colleagues and respond appropriately.**

   （1）_____

   （2）_____

   （3）_____

   （4）_____

   （5）_____

   （6）_____

2. **You will hear a short conversation about Mr. White coming to Mr. Zhang's office to say goodbye. In blanks 1 ~ 5，you should fill in a word，and in blanks 6 ~ 10，a sentence. Listen and fill in the blanks with the missing words or sentences.**

   （Mr. White，a businessman from America；Mr. Zhang，a Chinese businessperson）

   W：Good morning, Mr. Zhang, I've come to say _____ (1) to you. I've been here for a week, and I plan to go back home the day after tomorrow.

   Z：What a _____ (2) you are leaving so soon ! It seems like you only just got here! _____ (3) time _____ (4) ! I really wish you can stay here for a few more days.

   W：I'd like to, very much indeed. But I have some important business to attend to.

   Z：To be frank, Mr. White, we're very glad we've _____ (5) this transaction.

   W：_____ (6). In fact, it's been a pleasure doing business with you.

   Z：I also appreciate your attitude towards honoring contract.

   W：Now that we're got to know each other better, and I'm sure _____ _____ (7). Well, if possible may I ask you to express my thanks to your manager, Mr. Zhang? _____ (8).

   Z：OK, no problem. Have you got your tickets?

   W：Not yet. I can't speak Chinese. So would you do me a favor?

   Z：All right. I'll send the tickets to you this afternoon and _____ _____ (9).

W：＿＿＿＿＿＿＿＿＿＿＿＿＿＿＿＿＿（10）．

Z：You're welcome.

Culture Note

It is crucial① business manners to present gifts in many cases. It is essential to get to know the culture background when you present a gift to foreign guests.

Gift giving does not have to be a complicated process. With the proper research, an eye to cultural sensitivities and planning for the presentation, the chances of a cultural faux pas are greatly diminished②. Perhaps there is no other aspect of international business that varies as much on a country-by-country and culture-by-culture basis as gift-giving traditions. Here is a look at some of the cultural quirks③ involved in gift giving in regions where it is a regular practice.

Asia and the Pacific Tim

In most Asian cultures, gift giving remains an important aspect of the business relationship but failure to show up with tribute④ would not necessarily be a deal killer, especially if you are dealing with younger generations. Some cultural examples：

The "Red Envelope" is used exclusively⑤ for monetary presents in Sino-Asian cultures, especially around the Lunar New Year and at weddings. While once having no negative connotation⑥, the idea of the "Red Envelope" has now become synonymous with bribe-taking and bribe-giving⑦.

Four is considered an unlucky number.

Asians prefer gift-wrapping that is bright in color (red and gold are best). The more elaborate the wrapping, the better.

Generosity is appreciated and considered a sign of personal respect. Avoid presents that are grouped in four as this will bring bad luck to the receiver.

In the Islamic cultures of Asia, always give or receive gifts with the right hand only.

---

① crucial 决定性的；关键的

② diminish 减少；减损

③ quirk 怪癖

④ tribute 礼物；称赞

⑤ exclusively 专门地；排他地；仅仅

⑥ connotation 含义；言外之意

⑦ bribe-taking and bribe-giving 受贿和行贿

The Middle East and Africa

In most Arabic cultures gift giving is associated with the generosity and trust-worthiness of a firm or individual. Being generous in the Middle East is an important trait and is tied closely to the tenets of Islam and *the Koran*, the Islamic Holy Book. But here at least the visitor is somewhat off the hook; according to custom, it is the Arab host that will normally be the first to present a gift. In this region of the world reciprocity[1] is important. Giving a gift of lesser quality or expense than the one received is considered a personal slight, as is outdoing a host. Good gift ideas for this region of the world include: high-quality leather, silver, precious stones, crystal, and cashmere.

In Islamic cultures, gifts should never be accepted or presented with the left hand. When visiting the home of a Saudi colleague, men should not bring a gift especially for the hostess. It can be taken as an offense.

Compared to the Arabic cultures in the region, gifts in Israel are not so important. The attitude more resembles that found in North America; business is business; gifts are for holidays like Hanukkah.

South Arica is a mixture of business cultures and is best researched on a company-by-company basis.

Latin America

Gift giving in this part of the world is much less ritualistic compared to Asia and the Middle East, but it still plays an important part in the social culture. Not presenting a colleague with a small token of appreciation at the conclusion of a business deal is considered rude— but not fatal[2] to a business relationship. Most Latin American nations are high-context, relationship-driven cultures where gift giving underscores the value of business relations. Latin Americans simply appreciate and look favorably on individuals and companies that display thoughtfulness and generosity.

Gifts to women can easily be misconstrued[3] as a flirtation[4]. It should be made abundantly clear by content and presentation that no sexual innuendo is meant.

Avoid gifts when the receiver might feel compelled to wear or display unless you are very sure about his or her personal tastes.

---

① reciprocity 相互性；互惠主义
② fatal 致命的；毁灭性的
③ be misconstrued 被误解
④ flirtation 调情；挑逗

Pair Work

Student A:

1. You have been having a drink with some new friends. You need to go back to your hotel to do some work. You hope to see them again soon.

2. You are leaving work for the weekend. You meet a colleague on the way out.

3. You have got to know a man/woman on a training course. You have to leave now but would like to stay in touch.

Student B:

1. You have been having a drink with some new friends. You were expecting everybody to go on to a restaurant. One of the group announces he/she needs to go back to the hotel to do some work. You expect to see each other again soon.

2. You are leaving work for the weekend. You meet a colleague on the way out.

3. You have got to know a man/woman on a training course. He/she has to leave now but would like to stay in touch.

Socializing Practice

▶ Role-play

Situation: Mr. Black, an American businessman, has succeeded in concluding the business with Mr. Wang, the general manager in China Textile Import and Export Corporation, and will set up a joint venture in China and establish business relations with the company. His visiting China has achieved a lot. Now he has got ready to leave China and return to America. The general

manager sees him off at the airport.

Task for group of 2 or 4: Make a dialogue according to the given situation. There should be five different parts in your dialogue.

a. Seeing off at the airport

b. Confirming the business results

c. Giving a proper gift

d. Making an invitation

e. Wish a safe journey

Daily Practice

Tongue twister

1. I wish you were a fish in my dish.

我巴不得你是我碟中的鱼。

2. Double bubble gum bubbles double.

双重的泡泡糖能吹双重的泡泡。

3. Badmin was able to beat Bill at billiards, but Bill always beat Badmin badly at badminton.

巴德明在台球上能够打败比尔，但是打羽毛球时比尔常常大败巴德明。

4. How much wood would a woodcutter cut if a woodcutter could cut wood? He'd cut as much wood as a woodcutter could if a wood cutter could cut wood.

如果一个樵夫会砍木头的话，他砍多少木头？如果一个樵夫懂砍木头的话，他将像一个樵夫那样砍尽可能多的木头。

5. Moses supposes his toes are roses, but Moses supposes erroneously. For Moses, he knows his toes aren't roses as Moses supposes his toes to be!

摩西假设他的脚趾是玫瑰，但是摩西的假设错了。对摩西来说，他知道他的脚趾不是玫瑰，因为他只是假设他的脚趾是!

Read aloud

Don't Work for Money

The world is filled with smart, talented, educated and gifted people. We meet them every day. A few days ago, my car was not running well. I pulled it into a garage, and the young mechanic had it fixed in just a few minutes. He knew what was wrong by simply listening to the engine. I was amazed. The sad truth is, great talent is not enough.

I am constantly shocked at how little talented people earn. I heard the other day that less than 5 percent of Americans earn more than $100,000 a year. A business consultant who specializes in the medical trade was telling me how many doctors, dentists and chiropractors struggle financially. All this time, I thought that when they graduated, the dollars would pour in. It was this business consultant who gave me the phrase, "They are one skill away from great wealth." What this phrase means is that most people need only to learn and master one more skill and their income would jump exponentially. I have mentioned before that financial intelligence is a synergy of accounting, investing, marketing and law. Combine those four technical skills and making money with money is easier. When it comes to money, the only skill most people know is to work hard.

When I graduated from the US Merchant Marine Academy in 1969, my educated dad was happy. Standard Oil of California had hired me for its oil-tanker fleet. I had a great career ahead of me, yet I resigned after six months with the company and joined the Marine Corps to learn how to fly. My educated dad was devastated. Rich dad congratulated me.

Job security meant everything to my educated dad. Learning meant everything to my rich dad. Educated dad thought I went to school to learn to be a ship's officer. Rich dad knew that I went to school to study international trade. So as a student, I made cargo runs, navigating large freighters, oil tankers and passenger ships to the Far East and the South Pacific. While most of my classmates, including Mike, were partying at their fraternity houses, I was studying trade, people and cultures in Japan, Thailand, Singapore, Hong Kong, Vietnam, Korea and the Philippines. I also was partying, but it was not in any frat house. I grew up rapidly.

There is an old cliche that goes, "Job is an acronym for Just Over Broke." And unfortunately, I would say that the saying applies to millions of people. Because school does not think financial intelligence is intelligence, most workers "live within their means". They work and they pay the bills. Instead I recommend young people to seek work for what they will learn, more than what they will earn. Look down the road at what skills they want to acquire before choosing a specific profession and before getting trapped in the "Rat Race". Once people are trapped in the lifelong process of bill paying, they become like those little hamsters running around in those little metal wheels.

Their little furry legs are spinning furiously, the wheel is turning furiously, but come tomorrow morning, they'll still be in the same cage: great job.

When I ask the classes I teach, "How many of you can cook a better hamburger than McDonald's?" almost all the students raise their hands. I then ask, "So if most of you can cook a better hamburger, how come McDonald's makes more money than you?" The answer is obvious: McDonald's is excellent at business systems. The reason so many talented people are poor is because they focus on building a better hamburger and know little or nothing about business systems. The world is filled with talented poor people. All too often, they're poor or struggle financially or earn less than they are capable of, not because of what they know but because of what they do not know. They focus on perfecting their skills at building a better hamburger rather than the skills of selling and delivering the hamburger.

Appendix I   New Words and Expressions

Unit 1

resume：a summary of your personal information 简历

appearance：what sb./sth. appears to be 外貌，外表

personnel manager：the one who deals with employees 人事经理

adaptable：be able to adapt to a new situation 适应性强的

Mandarin：the official language of China 普通话

position：post 职位，岗位

enthusiasm：a feeling of excitement 热情

tolerant：showing respect for the opinions or practices of others 宽容的，容忍的

tactful：showing skills in dealing with people 机智的，老练的

notify：inform of something 通知

opportunity：chance 机会

responsibility：the condition or quality of being responsible 责任，职责

application：formal request 申请表，申请书

excusable：easily excused or forgiven 可辩解的，可原谅的

prospective：related to the future 预期的，未来的

achievement：a thing done successfully 成就，业绩

feedback：information about the results of a set of actions 回应，反馈

controversial：causing or likely to cause controversy 有争议的

derogatory remark：improper comment 贬损的评价

candidate：person who applies for a job 应聘者，候选人

show up：appear 露面，出现

recruit：take in 招收

curriculum vitae：resume 简历，履历

Korean Head Chef：the cook who is good at cooking Korean food 韩式料理首席厨师

prerequisite：something that is required in advance 先决条件

reputable cooking academy：famous cooking school or college 著名的烹饪院校

make a presentation：present something 演示，表演

cuisine：the practice or manner of preparing food 烹饪方法，菜肴

culinary arts：cooking skills 烹饪艺术，厨艺

formally：in a formal manner 正式地

argument：quarrel 争论，争吵

ambitious：having a strong desire for success 有雄心的

Melbourne Casino：a public building for entertainment in Melbourne 墨尔本娱乐城

dedication：selfless devotion 奉献精神

persuasive：convincing 有说服力的

stepping stone：a thing which is important in one's success 敲门砖，垫脚石

the office of teaching affairs：the department which is in charge of teaching 教务部门

acknowledgement：the act of expressing thanks for sb./sth. 感谢，致谢

Unit 2

appointment：a meeting arranged in advance 约会

report：announce one's presence 报到

staff：personnel who assist their superior in carrying out an assigned task 全体职员

emphasize：to stress, single out as important 强调，着重

creativity：the ability to create 创造性，创造力

description：a statement that represents something in words 描述，形容

consult：get or ask advice from 商议，商量

interrupt：interfere with someone else's activity 打断（别人的话等），阻止

delighted：greatly pleased 高兴的，欣喜的

accountant：someone who maintains and audits business accounts 会计人员，会计师

research：a search for knowledge 研究，追究

department：a specialized division of a large organization 部门，部

production：the act or process of producing something 生产，制作

appreciate：recognize with gratitude; be grateful for 感激，欣赏

guidance：something that provides direction or advice as to a decision or course of action 指导，引导

welcome aboard：welcome to join 欢迎加入

personnel：the department responsible for hiring and training and placing employees and for setting policies for personnel management 人事部门

purchasing：the act of buying 购买

Unit 3

superb：of surpassing excellence 极好的

luggage：a case used to carry belongings when traveling 行李

convenient：suited to your comfort or purpose or needs; easy to reach 方便的

surrounding：closely encircling（周围的）环境

security staff：those in an organization responsible for preventing spying or theft 保安

facilities：buildings, pieces of equipment, or services that are provided for a particular purpose 设备，设施

a joint venture：a venture by a partnership or conglomerate designed to share risk or expertise 合资企业

handle：be in charge of, act on, or dispose of 经营

amazing：surprising greatly 令人惊异的

Unit 4

uniform：clothing of distinctive design worn by members of a particular group as a means of identification 制服，军服

schedule：a temporally organized plan for matters to be attended to 进度表，时刻表

routine：an unvarying or habitual method or procedure 日常工作，例行公事

complicated：difficult to analyze or understand 结构复杂的，麻烦的

bulk：the property of something that is great in magnitude 大批的，大量的

presentation：a show or display; the act of presenting something to sight or view 陈述，报告

punishment：the act of punishing 惩罚

compatible：having similar disposition and tastes 相容的，和谐的

flatter：praise somewhat dishonestly 奉承，阿谀

sociable：inclined to or conducive to companionship with others 好交际的

apology：an expression of regret at having caused trouble for someone 道歉，认错

pressure：a force that compels 压（力）

apologize：acknowledge faults or shortcomings or failing 道歉，认错

efficiency：skillfulness in avoiding wasted time and effort 效率

professional：of or relating to a profession 专业的，专业性的

survival：a state of surviving; remaining alive 幸存，生存

achievement：the action of accomplishing something 完成，达到

enterprise：an organization created for business ventures 企（事）业单位，事业

involve：engage as a participant 包含，牵涉

admire：feel admiration for 赞赏，称赞

talented：endowed with talent or talents 有才能的，有才干的

bouncy：marked by lively action 快活的，精神的

eloquent：expressing yourself readily, clearly, effectively 雄辩的，有口才的

Unit 5

quality material：superior material 优良的材质

fine workmanship：exquisite workmanship 精湛的工艺

trial order：the first order for trial 试订单

bottom price：the lowest price 最低价

payment terms：terms of payment, methods of payment 支付方式

usual practice：routine ways of doing sth. 惯例

deposit：a payment given as a guarantee that an obligation will be met 存款；保证金

tie up：restrain from moving or operating normally 阻碍

to one's taste：to one's liking 合……口味

sole agency agreement：exclusive agency agreement 独家代理协议

annual：occurring or payable every year 每年的，一年的

turnover：the volume measured in dollars 营业额；成交量

Unit 6

reserve：book 预定

flight：a formation of aircraft 航班

depart：leave and start a journey to another place 离开，出发

round trip：a trip to some place and back again 双程

first class：the highest rank 头等舱

economy：cheap 经济的

fare：the moncy that you pay for a journey that you make 费用，票价

transfer：move from one place to another 转移

confirm：strengthen or make more firm 确认，证实

availability：something or someone you can find or obtain 可得到的东西（或人）

non-smoking：not allowed to smoke 无烟

offer：provide 提供

pick-up service：the service to pick someone up at the airport 接机服务

arrival：the act of arriving at a certain place 到达；抵达

confirmation：make sure something surely in a letter or on the telephone 确认

contract：a legal agreement 合同

be available：be free 有空

fix：decide upon 安排，决定（某事）

inform：let someone know something 通知，告知

sort out：solve the problem or organize the details 解决（问题）；理清（细节）

to the point：well to the purpose 中肯的，扼要的

upbeat：cheerful and hopeful 愉快的，高兴的

optimistic：hopeful about the future or the success 乐观的

Unit 7

seek for：look for 寻求

instruction：clear and detailed information on how to do something 说明书

essential：necessary 必要的

fax machine：a machine to send or receive the fax 传真机

copier：a machine which makes exact copies of writing or pictures on paper 复印机

printer：a machine that can make copies on paper of documents 打印机

scanner：a computer equipment that copies a picture or document onto a computer 扫描仪

paper shredder：a machine for shredding things such as documents 碎纸机

represent：take the place of 代表

arrange：plan, organize（an event）安排

in advance：ahead of time 提前

approximate：close to the correct number, time, or position 大概

operate：handle and cause to function 操作

complicated：difficult to analyze or understand 复杂的

button：a small object on a machine that you press in order to operate it 按钮

thermal paper：a kind of paper used in the printer 热敏纸

insert：put into something 插入

slot：a narrow opening in a machine or container 狭槽

adjust：change something so that it is more effective or appropriate 调整

signal：a series of radio waves which may carry information 信号

completion：a concluding action 完成

receipt：a piece of paper that you get from someone as proof that they have received money or goods from you 回执；收据

error：mistake 错误

template：a model or standard for making comparisons 模板

electronic：of or relating to electronics 电子的

serial number：a number on an object which identifies it 序列号

tray：a flat piece of wood, plastic, or metal, which usually has raised edges 托盘

paper jam：the paper jams the machine 卡纸

further：to a greater extent or degree 进一步的

attachment：a device that can be fixed onto a machine 附件

keep in touch：keep relation 保持联系

etiquette：a set of customs and rules for polite behaviour 礼仪

emergency：an unexpected and difficult or dangerous situation 紧急情况

faux pas：a socially awkward or tactless act 失礼；失言

Unit 8

intercourse：communication between individuals 交往；交流

strengthen：make strong or stronger 加强；变坚固

counterpart：a person or thing having the same function or characteristics as another 同仁

banquet：a meal that is well prepared and greatly enjoyed 宴会

troublesome：difficult to deal with 令人讨厌的，引起麻烦的

be occupied：be held or filled or be in use 被占用的，无暇抽身

make blunders：make mistakes 犯错误

hospitable：disposed to treat guests and strangers with cordiality and generosity 好客的；热情友好的

clumsy：lacking grace in movement or posture 笨拙的；复杂难懂的

pincer：a hand tool for holding consisting of a compound level for grasping 钳子，镊子

oblige sb. with sth.：provide a service of favor to someone 使满足，答应某人的请求

recreational activities：activities of or relating to recreation 娱乐活动

settle for：accept despite complete satisfaction 满足于

go in for：be interested in, like doing 从事；喜欢

amateur photography：to take or print photographs but lacking professional skill 业余摄影

buffet：a system of serving meals in which food is placed in a public area where the diners generally serve themselves 饮食柜台；快餐部；自助餐

random：lacking any definite plan or order or purpose 任意的；随机的

come to closing a deal：make an agreement 达成交易

be reinforced：be made stronger 加固；加强

subtle：delicate, not easy to notice, understand, or explain 微妙敏感的

smugness：an excessive feeling of self-satisfaction 装模作样；骄矜

superiority：advantage 优越（性），优等

exotic：introduced from another country; not native 外来的；异国的

repulsive：offensive to the mind 令人厌恶的；排斥的

revulsion：intense aversion 剧变；非常的厌恶

Unit 9

flexible attitude：the attitude that can be changed to suit new conditions 灵活的态度

shrugging one's shoulders：lift the shoulders slightly to show indifference or doubt 耸肩

typically：usually 通常地，典型地

intimate：being a very close relationship 亲密的

relative or acquaintance：a person related by blood or a friend 亲戚或熟人

social gathering：a gathering for the purpose of promoting fellowship 社交聚会

Bulgaria：a country in southeastern Europe 保加利亚

insult signal：impolite action 侮辱性质的行为

disrespectful：rude 无礼的

regulate：adjust 调节

acquiescence and approval：to agree or express agreement 默许与赞成

punctuality and promptness：the habit of timekeeping and doing things without delay 准时且迅速

representative：a person who represents others 代表

inquiry：request for help or information 询问

approach：come near 走进，靠近

supervisor：a person who supervises 主管

manage one's responsibility：do one's duty well 尽自己的责任

vehicle：conveyance such as a car and lorry used for transporting goods or people 机动车辆

by the roadside：beside the road 停在路旁

Unit 10

a homely dinner：a dinner which has a feeling of home，cozy and comfortable 家宴

token：a sign，indication of sth. 象征；标志

remind sb. of sth. 使某人想起某物

tempting：highly attractive and able to arouse hope or desire 诱惑人的

convey：make known ideas，views，feelings 表达，转达

deal：a particular instance of buying or selling 协定；交易

productive：producing good results；useful 富有成效的；有益的

crucial：of extreme importance 决定性的；关键的

diminish：make less；decrease；reduce 减少；减损

quirk：a strange attitude or habit 怪癖

tribute：sth. done，said，or given to show respect or admiration for sb. 礼物；称赞

exclusively：without any others being included or involved 专门地；排他地；仅仅

connotation：an idea that is implied or suggested 含义；言外之意

bribe-taking and bribe-giving：taking or giving illegal payments to in exchange for favors or influence 受贿和行贿

reciprocity：mutual exchange of commercial or other privileges 相互性；互惠主义

fatal：causing or resulting in death 致命的；毁灭性的

be misconstrued：be mistaken 被误解

flirtation：playful behavior intended to arouse sexual interest 调情；挑逗

Appendix II   Reference Answers

Unit 1

【Warming-up】

1. A well-designed resume, good communication skills, a graceful manner, to arrive on time, education background and work experience may contribute a lot to a successful interview.

2. Difficult questions and desirable answers:

(1) Why should we employ you?

Answer: The firm will benefit from my academic preparation, job skills, and enthusiasm about working.

(2) What are your greatest weaknesses?

Answer: I tend to drive myself too hard. / I expect others to perform beyond their capacities.

(3) Why do you leave your current job?

Answer: There is no room for the kind of career growth and advancement I would like.

(4) What kind of opportunities are you looking for?

Answer: I am looking for a company which recognizes and rewards hard work.

(5) What is your biggest accomplishment on the job?

Answer: I think it would have to be building team spirit among my co-workers.

【Listening Practice】

Task A:

1. F (She thinks there would be better chances for personal development.)

2. F (She has no experience for this job.)

3. T

4. F (She needs further training.)

5. T

Task B:

1. marketing department

2. thinks it would be a new challenge for her

3. work on weekends

4. thirty minutes to go there by bus

【Pair Work】

1. 1) It is possible to guess some questions of job interview but not all.

2) It is likely for some careful and responsible interviewers to do so. To an interviewee, honesty is the most important quality to a company.

3) It is up to the interviewer. Sometimes the interviewers consider that a person with a wonderful experience may have more confidence on their work.

4) In most circumstances, an applicant who uses the real examples in a job interview is considered to be honest and reliable.

5) Wearing a formal suit may bring a better first impression to the interviewers. But remember that the dressing should match with your personal disposition.

2. 1) I want to find a job as a sales manager because I like more challenge.

2) I may search the information of the company online and consult the acquaintances who work there to know more about the company. I also should know the requirement of the position I apply for.

3) I should show up with a tidy and clean dressing, several copies of resume and the optimistic attitude.

4) A handshake with short time and without too much power is more advocated by the westerners.

5) It is up to the culture of the interviewer. If he/she comes from Asia, maybe it is impolite to have eye-contact with him/her. But the western interviewers would prefer more eye-contact during talking.

6) It is a way of showing your respect to the interviewer. You may leave an impression to the interviewer that you care a lot for this position.

7) Think twice before answering these questions. On one hand you should be honest to answer the questions; on the other hand, you should notice that your answer will not bring a negative effect on you.

8) An applicant with a great enthusiasm for the job indicates that he/she cherishes the chance and has a great interest in the position.

3. 略

【Socializing Practice】

Task 1:

Tips for student A: You can ask some questions about the applicants' personal information, work experience, personality, expected salary and how long they would like to work here. The similar expressions and sentence structures of dialogue 1 and 2 may help you.

Tips for student B：

1. A list of subjects which the interviewer might ask probably includes the following items：personal information, work experience, expected salary, education background, your expected work hours and holidays, your loyalty to the company, some difficult questions and so on.

2. How to "sell" yourself at the interview? Here are some suggestions.

1）Highlight your advantages and loyalty to the company.

2）Answer the difficult questions in a reasonable way.

3）Give the evidence that you are hard-working and quick at learning.

Task 2：

Questions for Student A：（The owner of a Korean restaurant）

1. Could you introduce something about yourself?

2. What sort of work experience do you have?

3. Can you speak fluent English and Korean?

4. Have you got any qualified training or worked as a Korean Chef for years?

5. How would you describe your personality?

6. How long do you plan to stay at this city?

7. What is your opinion on working as a Korean Head Chef?

8. What's your expectation for the job?

Give a presentation to explain who you would like to hire and why.

Comparing with the four applicants, I probably would hire Tim Chung because she has ten years' experience in a Korean restaurant and has a great ambition to be a Head Chef. I think she would work hard to achieve her goal. Furthermore, she wants to move to Australia and stay a long time there, which may help to keep the stable running of my restaurant.

Tips for Student B：

Make a short self-introduction according to the given information. Answer the questions of student A in a reasonable way. The extra qualities as well as the given information will be constructive to your answers.

Task 3：略

Unit 2

【Listening Practice】

1. I'd better take this opportunity to explain to you exactly

2. Production, Personnel, Marketing and Finance

3. his title is the Production Manager

4. move to the Personnel

5. the secretaries in the department, will report to you

6. responsible for the Finance Department

【Pair Work】

Dialogue 1：

A：I'd like you to meet Mary, a new co-worker in our company.

B：Glad to meet you. Guess we'll be working together.

A：Yes. She'll be working closely with you. Could you show her around?

B：Sure, come with me, please.

Dialogue 2：

A：Hi, there. My name is Elbert.

B：You're new around here, right?

A：Yeah. I just started a couple of weeks ago.

B：Welcome to our company. If there is anything I can do for you, let me know.

A：Thanks. I'll appreciate that.

Dialogue 3：

A：Welcome to our board.

B：Thank you. I'm delighted to be working here. Shall I meet my colleagues?

A：Sure. Come with me. Mary, I would like you to meet our new co-worker, Jerry.
He just graduated from Guangzhou University.

C：Nice to meet you.

B：I am new to the working world. I would appreciate your guidance.

C：Well, I will try my best to assist you, if you need any help.

A：As the other guys are still not in, I will introduce you to them later.

B：OK.

Dialogue 4：

B：Ben, this is Angelina, your new co-worker.

C：Hi, Angelina, welcome to our board.

A：I'm happy to work with you.

C：Me too.

B：OK, now let's continue the tour and your introductions. Let's go to the second
floor. We can take the elevator over there. It'll be faster. This is Edward, our
accountant; and Paul, our cashier; and Meg, my secretary. This is Angelina,
our new employee.

D：Welcome to our group.

A：It's good to be here.

Unit 3

【Warming-up】

1. 略

2. Name, nationality, job.

Age, marriage position, religion.

3. It is an informal conversation about ordinary things or unimportant subjects or light conversation at a social event. We'd better be prepared and have some low-risk conversation openers ready.

4. Eye contact, facial expression, hand and upper-body movements, placement of arms and legs, distribution of weight, etc.

【Listening Practice】

1. A 2. B 3. A 4. C 5. A 6. C 7. B 8. C 9. A 10. C

【Pair Work】

1.

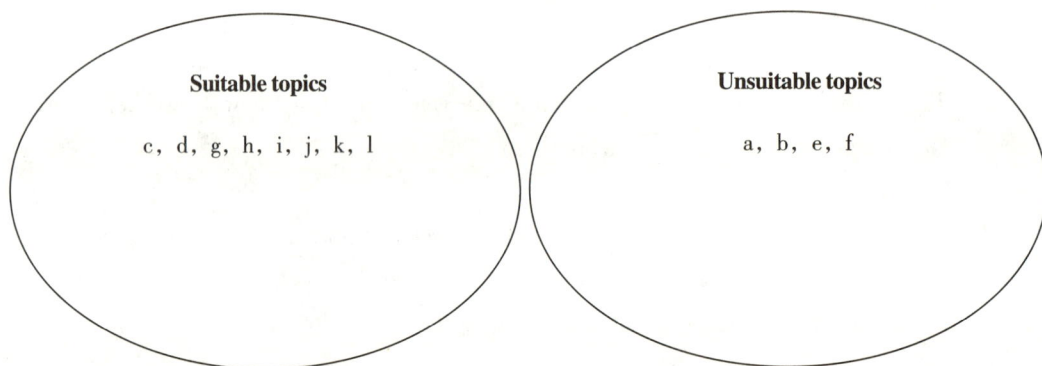

Suitable topics

c, d, g, h, i, j, k, l

Unsuitable topics

a, b, e, f

2.

Can	Can't
a, b, f, h	c, d, e, g, i, j

3.

A：Hello. May I help you with your luggage?

B：Thank you very much!

A：You are welcome. What's your name?

B：Helen. And yours?

A：Tom. I'm in International Trade department. What about you?

B: I'm in Business English. Where are you from?

A: I'm from France.

B: Oh, it is a very beautiful country!

A: Yes. In France there are many rivers, valleys, large cities—its scenery is beautiful. Would you describe your hometown?

B: I'm from Chaozhou. There are a lot of delicious local specialties. I hope you can visit Chaozhou someday.

A: I'd love to.

B: Here I am. This is my dormitory. Thank you very much for your help!

A: My pleasure! Goodbye!

B: Goodbye!

【Socializing Practice】
Situational Practice 1

What do you do?

How do you like Chinese food?

What do you usually do in your spare time?

Where did you buy your T-shirt? I like it very much.

What do you think of the football match last night?

Could you tell me about the concert last week?

Can you describe for me the weather in your country in this season?

Situational Practice 2

A: Good morning. Can I help you?

H: Yes, I have an appointment with Mr. Hansen at ten thirty.

A: May I have your name, please?

H: Paul Hunter, from the Huasheng International Trade Company.

A: Let me see... Oh, yes. Mr. Hunter, welcome to our company. But Mr. Hansen is at the meeting at this moment, and he'll finish it by ten thirty. Would you like to sit here to wait a moment?

H: OK, no problem.

A: Mr. Hunter, here's a cup of tea and some magazines for you. You may skim through them first.

H: Thank you.

Situational Practice 3

A：Hi! My name is Li.

B：Hi! My name is Jake. Nice to meet you, Li!

A：Nice to meet you, too, Jake. May I know which school you are from?

B：Yes, Nanhua Vocational School. Your school is beautiful.

A：Thank you! Welcome you here. What's your major?

B：Journalism. I want to be a journalist. What about you?

A：I'm doing Business English. Are you a new student?

B：Yes. This is my first year in this school.

A：Are you used to eating Chinese food here?

B：Sure. I like Chinese food and I'm learning to use chopsticks.

A：That's nice! What are your hobbies?

B：I like playing basketball. And you?

A：I like reading. In my spare time, I also like …

Unit 4

【Listening Practice】

1. forgive a green hand

2. how to deal with

3. should communicate with him

4. getting along with

5. respect the staff

6. partners

【Pair Work】

M：How is the project going?

T：Well, frankly speaking, I am running a little behind. It's 50% done.

M：Do you have any problem during the process? You should speed things up.

T：I have little chance to communicate with colleagues when I have problems. They are always too busy to help a green hand like me.

M：Have you ever helped others when they are in trouble? Most will give a hand to someone who has helped them.

T：I did. But I am so depressed because there is nobody that will help me.

M：And you should have good co-operation with other colleagues, you know a scientific schedule brings efficiency to the work.

T：I see your point, but I seem to be on bad terms with them.

M：Cheer up and pay more attention to your colleagues and the things will be much better. I am speaking from my experience.

T：Thank you so much.

M：And you should read as much as possible to enrich the knowledge.

T：That's a good idea. I can learn many useful things from books.

M：We're approaching the critical point for success or failure of this project; you'd better speed up and catch up with books.

T：Well，I will do it better.

M：If you have any problem in your work，let me know.

T：Thanks very much. I promise I will work harder.

经理：方案进行得怎么样了?

托尼：嗯，坦白说，我落后了一点，才完成了一半。

经理：在工作过程中有什么困难吗? 你应该加速了。

托尼：我遇到困难时很少有机会能和同事们交流。他们总是太忙了，不能帮一下我这个新手。

经理：他们有困难时你帮过他们吗? 人们大多都爱帮助曾经帮助过他们的人。

托尼：我帮过。但是我很苦恼的是没人愿意帮我。

经理：你应该和其他同事很好地合作，你要知道科学的时间进度表能提高工作效率。

托尼：我明白你的意思，但是我似乎和他们合不来。

经理：振作起来，多关注其他同事就会好很多的。这是我的经验之谈。

托尼：非常感谢。

经理：你也应该多读书，丰富知识。

托尼：是个好主意。从书上能学到很多有用的东西。

经理：我们正处在关系整个工程成败的关键时刻，你应该加速赶上其他人。

托尼：嗯，我会做得更好的。

经理：如果在工作中有什么困难，告诉我。

托尼：非常感谢，我一定会更加努力的。

Unit 5

【Warming-up】

1. Stay calm; listen; don't assume; explain clearly; speak clearly; ask for details; check and respond and so on.

2. We can tell our customers what we can do for them and persuade them to accept what we can provide. If we need to make some concessions to reach a deal，we may ask for more on other terms and conditions.

3. When we talk to people from different countries and areas，we need to change our negotiation style.

【Listening Practice】

1. 220   2. 3   3. 50   4. Hans   5. 123,467
6. 1979   7. 450   8. 19th   9. North   10. 35

【Pair Work】

1.

T：Mr. Zhang, we're quite interested in your Lady's dress Item No. 5065. We'd like to have your quotation.

Z：Well, our current quotation for this item is $ 25 per pc.

T：Mr. Zhang, we think your price is rather on the high side. We have received other offers for the same goods at much lower prices.

Z：But when we compare prices, we must take the quality into consideration.

T：Maybe the quality of your goods is superior. But the price difference should not be so large.

Z：Would you please tell us the quantity you're prepared to order from us?

T：We plan to place a trial order for 1,000 pcs.

Z：With a view to our long and friendly relations, we consider reducing our price by 5% if you can order 2,000 pcs. It leaves us with little profit at this price.

T：Well, let's meet each other half way. 8% discount for 2,000 pcs, OK?

Z：All right. Mr. Thomason, you really drive a hard bargain.

2.

C：Hello, Kary. I'd like to know whether the 600 air conditioners Item No. KY – 02 we ordered are available.

K：I was going to inform you about that. We're very sorry to tell you that the item you want is now out of stock. You see, there is a high demand for air conditioners due to the hot weather during the season.

C：That's too bad. Many of our customers are in urgent need of them.

K：Would you consider similar items we have recently produced? Especially Item No. KY – 03.

C：Is the quality as good as the one we've been ordering?

K：Even better! It's the same quiet as that one when it works, and it saves electricity better.

C：But...anyway, it's new to our market. I don't know whether our customers will like it or not.

K：Don't worry, Mr. Carpenter. This item sells well in many markets in your neighboring countries. I'm sure it will also be popular to your people.

C: That sounds great! Then maybe I'll begin with a trial order of 300 sets.

【Socializing Practice】

Situational Practice 1

K: It's a nice day, isn't it?

W: Yes. Lovely day. Is it so sunny during the whole season in this area?

K: Almost. It's usually bright for this time of the year here. Mr. White, we've reserved one room for you at Dahua Hotel. It's one of the best hotels in Guangzhou.

W: Oh, thank you very much, Kary! How far is it to the hotel?

K: About 30 minutes by taxi.

W: Good.

K: Mr. White, is it the first time for you to Guangzhou?

W: Right, the first time. It's a large city, isn't it?

K: Yes. There are over 16 million people in Guangzhou.

W: Wah, so many!

K: Also, Guangzhou is a historic and commercial center in South China. There are a lot of places of interest, different local specialties and a number of economic zones. Many foreigners have invested here.

W: Oh, I hope to know more about this beautiful city.

K: You will, I'm sure.

Situational Practice 2

K: Good morning, can I help you?

F: Good morning, Kary. I call for the 3,000 sets of cameras under Order No. LJ 212.

K: Is there anything wrong with it?

F: Unfortunately, we've found that the model is not the one we want.

K: Oh, I'm sorry to hear that. I'll check it right now. Please wait a moment.

…

K: Yes. I'm sorry, Mr. Frank. Our factory made a mistake and sent a wrong delivery when they packed the goods. I'm really sorry!

F: But the problem is that our customer is waiting for the complete order. Can you send us the replacements immediately?

K: Sure, Mr. Frank. We'll send the right order on the first available ship. And could you do us a favour to find a new buyer for the wrong goods?

F: Maybe I can try. Then how about the discount?

K: We can allow 15% discount on the original price.

F：OK. I'll try my best.

Situational Practice 3

C：Mr. Deng, can you tell me with which company you will arrange the insurance on our cargo?

D：Sure. We always insure our goods with the People's Insurance Company of China as per their Ocean Marine Cargo Clause.

C：As I know, PICC is the biggest insurance company in China, isn't it?

D：You are right. It offers very good services.

C：Then what risks do you usually cover?

D：We usually cover All Risks for our goods. All Risks cover W. P. A. plus general additional risks, including theft, pilferage & non-delivery risks, fresh water and/ or rain damage risks, clash and breakage risks etc.

C：Does All Risks include War Risk and Strike Risk. We'd like to cover these risks too.

D：No. War Risk and Strike Risk are special additional risks, and they have to be arranged separately.

C：Then do remember to cover them for us.

D：No problem. But they are subject to additional premiums, because our CIF quotation doesn't include there risks.

C：OK. One more point, what's the insurance amount? And when and where is the claim payable?

D：According to the international usual practice, we insure for 110% of the invoice value. The claim can be payable at the place of destination within 45 days after the arrival of the goods.

C：All right. Thank you very much!

Unit 6

【Listening Practice】

1. B   2. A   3. A   4. B   5. A   6. B   7. C   8. C

【Pair Work】

Pair Work 1：

A：Good morning. What can I do for you?

B：Yes, I'd like to make a reservation to Beijing.

A：When do you want to fly?

B：As soon as possible.

A：OK, now it's 9：20. We have 5 flights in the morning. What time do you prefer?

The earliest one is full. Then there is a flight in 10: 45, but it is more expensive than others. Is it OK?

B: Never mind. It's OK.

A: Which would you prefer, first class or economy?

B: Economy class, please.

A: OK, sir, let me check. CA1310, departs at 10: 45 a. m. , economy class.

B: Right. Thanks very much!

A: It's my pleasure.

Pair Work 2:

A: Good morning. This is Linda speaking. What can I do for you?

B: Good morning. I'm Mary. I want to make an appointment with you. Can we meet on Tuesday afternoon?

A: Let me check my schedule. Please wait for me several seconds.   (after several seconds) Sorry for keeping you waiting. I'm sorry I am not free at that time.

B: Never mind. I will be free on Wednesday afternoon. Is it suitable?

A: OK, good to me. So I will go to your company at 2 o'clock on Wednesday.

B: Yes, I will be expecting you.

A: Wonderful. Thanks very much.

B: You are welcome. Goodbye.

A: Goodbye.

Unit 7

【Listening Practice】

1. fax machine   2. copier   3. four   4. telephone   5. how   6. When
7. couple   8. three   9. buttons   10. transfer   11. people   12. computer
13. trouble   14. 100   15. programs   16. PowerPoint   17. e-mail

【Pair Work】

Task 1

A: Good morning, can I help you?

B: Good morning. Is this _____ (company's name)?

A: Yes, it is.

B: That's good. I'm here to meet Mr. Williams.

A: Do you have an appointment?

B: No, I don't.

A: Could you tell me what company you are representing?

B: I'm _____ (name) from _____ (company's name).

A: Can I ask what you wish to see him about?

B：I want to introduce the development of a new computer technology to Mr. Williams. This technology is very useful for your company's business.

A：Thank you for your timely notification. I'm so sorry that he has been away on business for this week.

B：What a pity! But this technology is really very useful for your company.

A：Would you please tell me your telephone number and leave your introduction material so I can ring you up to arrange an appointment?

B：That's a good idea. Thanks you very much!

A：It's my pleasure.

Task 2：

  __3__ → __8__ → __6__ → __2__ → __7__ → __4__ → __5__ → __1__

The original dialogue：

A：Did you put this morning's faxes on my desk? I'm waiting for some urgent faxes from headquarters. I'm pretty sure they came in last night.

B：Everything that came in the office fax machine last night is all on your desk, but I noticed that some of the faxes came through pretty blurred. Maybe you take a look at them if the copy is unreadable. I'll call them and ask them to refax.

A：Yeah, you're going to have to call them and get them to be refaxed. These copies are so dark. I can't make out any of the words.

B：What about that one?

A：This one? This one is so light that I can barely read it. How can that be?

B：You know, I think the fax machine is out of toner. I can change the toner cartridge. That should solve the problem.

A：Yes, but this one will have to be refaxed as well. And look, there's about 3 pages missing. It looks like the fax machine ate half of my important faxes, and ones that made it through are so blurred or too light. They are unreadable.

B：I guess the fax machine is out of paper too. Don't worry, I'll have someone look at it this afternoon, and in the meantime, I'll have your documents refaxed to our other fax machine.

Unit 8

【Listening Practice】

1. a) a concert, play or show

b) doesn't go in for concert

c）略

2. a) an informal gathering then a meal in a restaurant

b) has to attend an urgent meeting

c）略

2．（1）refers to　（2）in order to　（3）dinner　（4）sporting events

（5）concerts or company events

（6）Careful planning is necessary

（7）you should get some idea of the client's personal interests

（8）Still another thing you should consider is the cost

（9）helps you achieve your business objectives

（10）makes your clients enjoy themselves

【Pair Work】

Task 1

1．How nice of him. I'll be delighted to go.

2．I regret to inform you that owing to a previous engagement, we shall not be able to come.

3．Thank you. That's very kind of you. I'll certainly wait for you in front of the hotel gate.

4．It's very kind of you to have invited me. People have always told me that the Chinese are very hospitable. Now, I've seen it with my own eyes.

5．To the health of all present, to our friendships and cooperation. Bottoms up.

6．Thanks. You needn't worry about me. I won't miss anything.

7．Thank you for giving a dance party, Mr. A. I think we'll have a good time.

8．Oh, we have many entertainment activities. Sometimes we go to the movies. Sometimes we go to the concert. Young people like popular songs and dancing. I usually go to play golf.

9．I'm very glad you have enjoyed yourself tonight. You are welcome to our dance hall again.

【Socializing Practice】

A：Good morning, Mr. Smith. I'm afraid there's been a change in today's dinner arrangement. I just got word that your appointment with our director will have to be put off.

B：Oh, no problem.

A：Mr. Michael is sending his apologies and has asked whether it is convenient to change the dinner time?

B：I certainly have no objection.

A：Will tomorrow suit you? Shall we make it 6：30 tomorrow afternoon?

B：OK. That's settled. Well, I will have more free time today and I can do some shopping. I'd like to get some souvenirs to take back to my friends at home.

Unit 9

【Warming-up】

1. Picture 1 "Let's keep our fingers crossed" in the United States, England, and Sweden means that the person is hoping for good luck. But in Greece and Turkey it means the breaking of a friendship, and in parts of Italy it means "OK".

Picture 2 is normally used when talking privately about a third person, meaning that person is crazy, often in a joking way.

Picture 3 indicates "I have no idea." or "I don't know."

The gesture in Picture 4 means that "I can't / didn't hear you."

Picture 5 means "That's enough. It's all over for me."

In Picture 6 the "thumbs down" sign indicates "refusal", "defeat" or "no good" or "bad news" to Americans.

2. Smile; eye-contact; gesture; facial expressions; dressing; distance between each other etc.

3. (1) T   (2) T   (3) T   (4) F   (5) F   (6) F

【Listening Practice】

Task A：1. F 2. T 3. F 4. T 5. F

Task B：

1. nodding the head up and down

2. should not stand too close, your hands a little open

3. In Asian and South American

【Pair Work】

1. 1) English people do not usually stand very close to others. They shake hands to strangers and new friends, and embrace and kiss their good friends.

2) If you are from France, you often keep a short distance. You may shake hands and even kiss others.

3) If you are from Japan, you will keep a long distance and bow to each other.

4) If you are from Jordan, you often stand very close to others and like to shake others' hands all the time.

5) If you are from China, you will keep a medium distance (not too long or too short) and incline to shake hands to others.

2. 略

【Socializing Practice】

▶ Role-play

Task 1：略

Task 2:

I would say that he has to be more friendly and welcoming to the customers and could politely told the person on the phone to please hold for a moment and that he should be more enthusiastic about his job.

Task 3:

He could/should have looked up, smiled at you and at least nodded a greeting.

Task 4:

If his conversation continued too long, he should have politely placed his caller on hold and inquired as to the customer's needs, asked someone else to assist the customer or advised the customer how long he would be.

▶ Discussion

Some jobs may use a lot of body language such as teachers, doctors, receptionists and dancers and so on.

▶ Assignment after class

1. It is widely used in the US to mean "Great, perfect, acceptable, OK". But in Belgium and France, it means "zero"; in Tunisia, it is used as a threat.

2. To Chinese, it's a sign of telling somebody to come closer while it means waving goodbye for Americans.

3. It means absent-minded or lacking interest.

4. It means "Oh, I forgot." or an expression of surprise.

5. It means "Slow down, relax or wait a second."

Unit 10

【Listening Practice】

1. (1) Thank you for saying so. You've all been very kind. / You've all made me very welcome.

(2) That's nice of you to say so. I'm sad to go, too, but I'm sure we'll be seeing each other again soon.

(3) I will. And give us a ring if you're ever in …

(4) Yes, thank you.

(5) Don't worry. I won't forget.

(6) I hope so.

2. (1) goodbye   (2) pity   (3) How   (4) flies   (5) concluded

(6) It's the result of our joint efforts

(7) we can do more business to our mutual benefit

(8) Thank him for entertaining me with such great hospitality

(9) I'll come to see you off at the airport

(10) Thank you for being so considerate

【Pair Work】

1.

B：It's time to have dinner. Why don't we go to a famous restaurant to have a big meal together? I know it well. Let's go!

A：Oh, I'd like to go with you, but I have to go back to the hotel to deal with some important papers first. It's very urgent.

B：That's a pity. But work must come first. Hope to see you soon.

A：OK. Thank you. Wish you a wonderful time, everybody. Goodbye.

2.

A：Hello, Michael. It's so happy to meet you at this moment. Do you have any plans for this weekend?

B：Yes. My wife and I will make a short trip to Hainan Island.

A：Oh, that sounds great! Have a nice weekend!

B：The same to you. Goodbye.

3.

A：Hello, Mary. It is a great honor to be your friend and to study with you.

B：I also feel so.

A：What a pity it is that we have to separate. Can I keep in touch with you in the future?

B：Of course. Here is my business card.

A：OK. Thank you. Here is mine. Hope to see you again soon.

B：Me too. Goodbye. Wish you a nice trip.

【Socializing Practice】

A：All my bags are checked in. I believe I am all set to go.

B：You must be excited to go home after such a long business trip. I hope you have a good time in Beijing.

A：Sure I am. I do have a wonderful time. So, we will be expecting the first shipment in less than a month.

B：Yes, that's right. They will be delivered as soon as possible.

A：Good. I think all the goods will be selling very well in my country.

B：I hope so. It is good to work with you. I want to thank you for placing such a big order with us. You won't be disappointed.

A：I am sure I won't. I really appreciate you for your hospitality.

B：It is my pleasure. Here is a small gift for you as a token of our friendship and business.

A: How beautiful it is! What is it?

B: It is a beautiful piece of embroidery (刺绣). The pattern is phoenix which is a kind of bird symbolizing good luck and harmony in Chinese culture.

A: Thanks a lot. I will treasure it all my life. It is the first time I have seen the Chinese embroidery. It is splendid.

B: I am glad you like it. It just stands for our friendship. I am looking forward to seeing you again.

A: Welcome you to Canada for business. There I will invite you to taste delicious Canadian food and act as a guide for you to enjoy the beautiful scenery in Canada.

B: Thank you very much for saying so. If there is a chance, I will consider that.

A: It's very nice of you to come and see me off.

B: Take care of yourself and have a nice flight. Please keep in touch.

A: Sure I will.

Appendix III   Listening Scripts

Unit 1

【Listening Practice】

You are going to listen to two conversations about job interview and finish task A and B.

Conversation 1

M: Why are you interested in our company?

W: Your company is world famous, so I think there will be better chances for personal development.

M: You're right. Do you think you have the appropriate qualifications for this job?

W: Sure. My qualifications meet your job description.

M: But you have no experience for this job.

W: That is true. But I'm eager to learn and also quick at learning.

M: Since you need further training, are you familiar with the trainee salary?

W: No. What is the monthly salary?

M: 800 *yuan* per month. Do you mind if I give you an answer tomorrow?

W: Not at all.

Conversation 2:

(I = Interviewer, K = Kary)

I: Hi, Kary, please take a seat.

K: Thank you.

I: We are now considering your application. Are you interested in working in the marketing department?

K: Yes, I'm very interested in marketing; it would be a new challenge for me.

I: How do you feel about working on weekends?

K: Working on weekends? I haven't thought about it, but I would definitely consider it.

I: People in that department often need to do market surveys during the weekends.

K: Then I would try my best to do that.

I: By the way, do you live far from the company?

K: No, it only takes me thirty minutes to get here by bus.

I: That's fine. Thank you.

Unit 2

【Listening Practice】

Listen to the following conversation and complete the sentences.

A: Good morning, Helen Wright. I think I'd better take this opportunity to explain to you exactly who's who in the company. You'll need to know who to go to when you want to contact a particular manager. Let's start right from the top. David Clinton is the Manager Director. His Personal Assistant is Ruth Rice. The company is divided into four departments: Production, Personnel, Marketing and Finance, clear?

B: Yes.

A: Right. George Brown looks after Production, and his title is the Production Manager. George Lewis works as Personal Assistant in the Production Department. Then there are two secretaries. Is that clear?

B: Yes.

A: Now let's move to the Personnel. We've got Lisa Leslie here, and her title is Personnel Manager.

B: I see.

A: And Jane Williams works for Lisa Leslie as Personal Assistant. And then there are two secretaries in the department, clear?

B: Yes. Thank you.

A: As you know, I'm the Marketing Manager. And for the next five months you'll work as my Personal Assistant. Judy Miller and Becky Parker, the secretaries in the department, will report to you. Then finally, Ray Allen is responsible for the Finance Department. His PA is Cartier Martin. There are three secretaries in the department. I think you met them yesterday, right?

B: Yes.

Unit 3

【Listening Practice】

Listen to the recording and select the correct answer for each sentence, which may be missing one or more words.

1. What's your name?
2. Where do you live?
3. How's it going?
4. Where does she work?

5．Where are they from?

6．How many people are there in your family?

7．Hey, what's new?

8．What does he do?

9．What do you do in your spare time?

10．What does your father do for a living?

Unit 4

【Listening Practice】

Listen to the following conversation and complete the sentences.

C：I can't stand that stupid guy any longer. He's unbelievable.

B：Oh, my dear lady, take it easy. You should forgive a green hand like him.

C：He does everything so mindlessly, he is going to drive me crazy.

B：I suggest you talk with him and teach him how to deal with problems properly.

C：I've told him how to do that several times, but he's never listened to me.

B：Maybe you should communicate with him just like a friend, not a boss.

C：Oh, I always have difficulty in getting along with the staff.

B：Just treat them as your good friends and talk with them as we do. Make sure you don't lose your temper!

C：Oh, that's tough. I'm afraid I'll have to change my image.

B：No, that's not necessary. Just respect the staff and their own opinions.

C：But sometimes they offer some useless proposals, awfully useless.

B：Well, no one is perfect.

C：That's right. I should speak to them politely.

B：All men are equal in the eyes of the God. We are all equal partners in the team.

C：Thanks very much. You're really eloquent.

B：Thanks for saying that.

Unit 5

【Listening Practice】

You will hear 10 short sentences. Fill in the corresponding blanks according to what you've heard.

（1）The price of Pure Cotton Bed Sheet is US $ 220 per dozen.

（2）They will lower their price by 3 percent.

（3）Soda has a history of more than 50 years.

(4) The applicant for Sales Administrator is Mr. Hans.

(5) The net weight of the goods is 123, 467 kilograms.

(6) The first branch of the BC Company started in 1979.

(7) If you pay in Renminbi, the price is RMB 450 *yuan.*

(8) The last day for Mr. Lee to stay is 19th December.

(9) The sender of the parcel is Fred North.

(10) 35 percent of the balance will be paid in local currency.

Unit 6

【Listening Practice】

You are going to hear 3 conversations. As you listen, decide which answer is correct.

Conversation 1

M: I'd like to book a seat on the 8:30 flight to New York on 1st July.

W: I'm sorry, sir, that flight is fully booked.

M: Oh, well, in that case I'll go on the 10:30.

W: Yes, sir, we have seats on that flight.

Conversation 2

M: Good evening, Caesar's Place. How may I help you?

W: I would like to make a reservation for two at 7:00 p. m.

M: Your last name, please?

W: Norton.

M: Would you like smoking or non-smoking seats?

W: Non-smoking. Can I have a table by the window?

M: No problem, madam. Thank you very much.

Conversation 3

(H = Hotel, C = Caller, R = Reservations)

H: Grand Park Hotel, good afternoon. Can I help you?

C: Good afternoon. Yes, I'd like to inquire whether there are two double rooms available from 20th June to 25th June.

H: Just a minute-I'll put you through to reservations.

R: Reservations, Mrs. Elbe speaking.

C: Mercado, Eleanor Mercado speaking. I'd like to know whether there are two double rooms available from 20th June for 5 nights.

R: Let's have a look. Well, there is one available with a balcony and one without a balcony.

C：That's fine. What other amenities does the room offer?

R：There is a satellite TV, coffee and tea making facilities, a bathrobe and bath slippers, a separate toilet and shower cubicle, and 24h room service. You can choose between a queen size bed or twin beds.

C：The room with a balcony should be equipped with a queen size bed, the other one with twin beds, please.

R：OK, how do you spell your name, please?

C：M-E-R-C-A-D-O.

R：Thank you. Bed and breakfast or half board?

C：We only take breakfast.

R：Will you be paying by credit card?

C：Yes, visa, my number is 6228 4700 12549.

R：Thanks, please let me know your mail address or fax for you to sign it. Then please fax it back to us.

C：Please mail it to emercado@ email. com.

R：Thanks. We are looking forward to seeing you here.

C：Goodbye.

R：Goodbye.

Unit 7

【Listening Practice】

You are going to hear Kary speaking about being a receptionist, please fill in the blanks while listening.

Obviously we use a fax machine, a copier, and printers; I think we have about four different printers in this office that I use on a daily basis. I also use a telephone system. Sometimes those can be pretty complicated. You've got to really know how to use it. They often come with a manual. When we had our telephone system replaced here a couple months ago, I actually had to spend about three hours going through the manual figuring out how to program it, figuring out how to program everyone else's buttons, intercom buttons, things like that. You've got to know how to transfer a phone call. Really, that's your main job, being a front line phone person for transferring calls to voice mail or other people, jobs like that. Also you've got to know how to use a computer. If you don't know how to use a computer, you're in trouble because I will tell you 100% of receptionist and secretarial positions require PC knowledge. You've got to know how to use basic programs such as those in Microsoft Office: Excel, PowerPoint, Word and Outlook which is a big one for e-mail.

Unit 8

【Listening Practice】

1. Listen to the recording of two short extracts, where hosts invite their visitors to take part in a social activity. The invitations are rejected.

(H = Host, V = Visitor)

Extract 1

H: I was wondering if we could make arrangements for you when you come over.

V: That would be very nice. What do you have in mind?

H: Would you be free on Monday evening? If you like we could do something together. Well, we could go to see a concert or a play—or go to a show, of some kind?

V: I don't really go for concerts. They make me fall asleep. I think the theatre would be more interesting. I'd like that.

H: Oh, that's good. We'll do that then. I'll find out exactly what's on, then I'll call you.

Extract 2

H: ...and then tonight we've planned a little gathering here, an informal get-together, if you'd like to join us. You'll meet some of our other colleagues, then we plan to go out for dinner together—to a well-known restaurant. I don't know if you have any other plans this evening?

V: Oh, it is tempting. I'd really like to, but I have an urgent meeting to attend. Thank you all the same.

H: That's a pity. Hope you can attend our activity next time.

2. You will hear a short conversation about entertaining a client. In blanks 1 ~ 5, you should fill in a word or phrase, and in blanks 6 ~ 10, a sentence. Listen and fill in the blanks with the missing words or sentences.

Entertaining a Client

Corporate hospitality refers to the ways in which companies entertain their customers in order to gain business. Entertaining clients or customers is quite common in the business world. Companies treat their clients to dinner, sporting events, concerts or company events in order to bring up the matter of business in a social setting. Social events like these can not only make business talk easier, but also help further develop relationships with the clients. But, of course, entertaining clients at random can be a waste of both time and money. Careful planning is necessary. First of all, you should be clear about what business objectives you want to achieve. This may help you decide on the right form of entertainment.

You can not possibly have any intimate discussions while watching a football game. Second, you should get some idea of the client's personal interests. If you treat your client to something he or she dislikes, you are certainly wasting your money! Still another thing you should consider is the cost. Although it is the company that covers all the expenses, you still have to be economical. A successful entertainment is one that helps you achieve your business objectives and makes your clients enjoy themselves.

Unit 9

【Listening Practice】

You are going to listen to a passage about body language and finish task A and B.

Body language shows all kinds of feelings, wishes and attitudes and is sometimes as important as spoken language.

A smile is the commonest facial expression. It is intended to show your friendliness to other people.

In most countries, nodding the head up and down shows agreement, while shaking the head means that you do not agree, or that you refuse to do something.

If you stand holding your arms across your chest, you may be protecting yourself—like from a conversation talk you do not want to have! If you sit looking at and turn toward the person you are talking to, it shows that you are interested. If you roll your eyes and turn your head away, most likely you do not believe what you are hearing, or you do not like what you hear.

We show respect for people by using different gestures. It is probably not a good idea to give a hug to your boss or to your teacher. You should not stand too close to him or her and should stand with your hands a little open to show that you are willing to listen.

There are differences in body language in different places. In Asian and South American countries, children are taught that looking directly at an adult is not polite behaviour. However, some teachers in North America punish students who do not look them in the eye because they think they are not telling the truth.

Unit 10

【Listening Practice】

1. Put yourself in the position of a visitor leaving after a short stay. Listen to these remarks made by your new colleagues and respond appropriately.

1) It's been a pleasure having you with us.

2) On behalf of the group, I'd like to say how sad we are to see you go.

3) You've got our number, so please stay in touch.

4) Have you got everything?

5) So, make sure you remember to drive on the left!

6) See you soon.

2. You will hear a short conversation about Mr. White coming to Mr. Zhang's office to say goodbye. In blanks 1 ~ 5, you should fill in a word, and in blanks 6 ~ 10, a sentence. Listen and fill in the blanks with the missing words or sentences.

W: Good morning, Mr. Zhang, I've come to say goodbye to you. I've been here for a week, and I plan to go back home the day after tomorrow.

Z: What a pity you are leaving so soon! It seems like you only just got here! How time flies! I really wish you can stay here for a few more days.

W: I'd like to, very much indeed. But I have some important business to attend to.

Z: To be frank, Mr. White, we're very glad we've concluded this transaction.

W: It's the result of our joint efforts. In fact, it's been a pleasure doing business with you.

Z: I also appreciate your attitude towards honoring the contract.

W: Now that we're got to know each other better, and I'm sure we can do more business to our mutual benefit. Well, if possible may I ask you to express my thanks to your manager, Mr. Zhang? Thank him for entertaining me with such great hospitality.

Z: OK, no problem. Have you got your tickets?

W: Not yet. I can't speak Chinese. So would you do me a favor?

Z: All right. I'll send the tickets to you this afternoon and I'll come to see you off at the airport.

W: Thank you for being so considerate.

Z: You're welcome.

Bibliography

［1］Ju A C. 商务英语情景口语 100 主题［M］. 北京：外文出版社，2007.

［2］李进. 英语［M］. 北京：化学工业出版社，2008.

［3］沈爱珍. 新编商务英语听力：第 2 册［M］. 北京：高等教育出版社，2011.

［4］奥伯. 现代商务沟通［M］. 北京：中国人民大学出版社，2009.

［5］罗伯茨，布鲁斯，黄智颖. 商务英语沟通［M］. 上海：复旦大学出版社，2011.

［6］占俊英. 跨文化商务沟通［M］. 北京：北京理工大学出版社，2013.

［7］方国爱，徐芳. 职场沟通英语［M］. 杭州：浙江大学出版社，2012.

［8］劳斯. 商务谈判技巧［M］. 北京：人民邮电出版社，2008.

［9］马龙海. 新视野商务英语视听说［M］. 北京：外语教学与研究出版社，2006.

［10］王乃彦. 外贸英语口语［M］. 北京：对外经济贸易大学出版社，2000.

［11］邬孝煜，彭青龙. 国际商务英语［M］. 上海：上海交通大学出版社，2000.

［12］诸葛霖. 外贸英语对话［M］. 北京：对外经济贸易大学出版社，1998.

［13］中国国际贸易学会商务专业培训考试办公室. 全国国际商务英语考试（一级）大纲与复习指南［M］. 北京：中国商务出版社，2012.

［14］全国国际商务专业人员职业资格考试指定用书编委会. 国际商务英语口语［M］. 北京：中国对外经济贸易出版社，2003.

［15］王墩田，肖建壮. 全国公共英语等级考试必备：二级［M］. 苏州：苏州大学出版社，2009.

［16］蔡昕. 文秘英语［M］. 北京：高等教育出版社，2007.

［17］英国柯林斯公司. 柯林斯高阶英汉双解词典［Z］. 姚乃强，等译. 北京：商务印书馆，2008.

［18］廖瑛. 实用商务公关英语：口语［M］. 北京：机械工业出版社，2008.

［19］Comfort J. 牛津商务英语教程：成功交际［M］. 上海：复旦大学出版社，2001.

［20］Michellc J. International Business Culture［M］. 上海：上海外语教育出版社，2002.

［21］Mitchell C. 国际商业文化［M］. 上海：上海外语教育出版社，2004.

［22］常俊跃. 跨文化交际［M］. 北京：北京大学出版社，2011.

［23］刘乃银. 英语泛读教程：第 3 册［M］. 北京：高等教育出版社，2010.

［24］全国中小学教材编写组. 初中英语：9［M］. 上海：上海教育出版社，2009.

[25] http://www. doc88. com/p – 079841040705. html

[26] http://wenku. baidu. com/view/066e385fbe23482fb4da4cb9. html

[27] http://wenku. baidu. com/view/2a4b54c3d5bbfd0a7956738b. html

[28] http://wenku. baidu. com/view/22c0604be45c3b3567ec8bb4. html